LILIOM

LILIOM

COPYRIGHTED, 1921, BY
UNITED PLAYS INC.

All rights reserved

First Printing..........May, 1921
Second "   ....June, 1921

CAUTION—All persons are hereby warned that the plays published in this volume are fully protected under the copyright laws of the United States and all foreign countries, and are subject to royalty, and any one presenting any of said plays without the consent of the Author or his recognized agents, will be liable to the penalties by law provided. Applications for the acting rights must be made to the United Plays, Inc., 1428 Broadway, New York City.

Printed in the United States of America

LILIOM

A LEGEND IN SEVEN SCENES
AND A PROLOGUE

BY
FRANZ MOLNAR

ENGLISH TEXT AND INTRODUCTION BY
BENJAMIN F. GLAZER

BONI AND LIVERIGHT
PUBLISHERS   NEW YORK

As originally produced by The Theatre Guild, on the night of April 20, 1921, at the Garrick Theatre, New York City.

CAST OF CHARACTERS

(In the order of their appearance)

Marie .... Hortense Alden
Julie .... Eva Le Gallienne
Mrs. Muskat .... Helen Westley
"Liliom" .... Joseph Schildkraut
"Liliom" is the Hungarian for lily, and the slang term for "a tough"

Four Servant Girls ....
{
Frances Diamond
Margaret Mosier
Anne de Chantal
Elizabeth Parker
}

Policemen .... {
Howard Claney
Lawrence B. Chrow
}

Captain .... Erskine Sanford
Plainclothes Man .... Gerald Stopp
Mother Hollunder .... Lilian Kingsbury
"The Sparrow" .... Dudley Digges
Wolf Berkowitz .... Henry Travers
Young Hollunder .... William Franklin
Linzman .... Willard Bowman
First Mounted Policeman .... Edgar Stehli
Second Mounted Policeman .... George Frenger
The Doctor .... Robert Babcock
The Carpenter .... George Frenger
First Policeman of the Beyond .... Erskine Sanford
Second Policeman of the Beyond ..... Gerald Stopp

CAST OF CHARACTERS (Continued)

The Richly Dressed Man ....Edgar Stehli
The Poorly Dressed Man ....Philip Wood
The Old Guard ....Walton Butterfield
The Magistrate ....Albert Perry
Louise ....Evelyn Chard
Peasants, Townspeople, etc.
    Lela M. Aultman, Janet Scott, Marion M. Winsten, Katherine Fahnestock, Lillian Tuchman, Ruth L. Cumming, Jacob Weiser, Maurice Somers, John Crump.

Prologue
    An Amusement Park on the Outskirts of Budapest
First Scene ....A Lonely Place in the Park
Second Scene. The Tin Type Shop of the Hollunders
Third Scene ....The Same
Fourth Scene
       A Railroad Embankment Outside the City

Intermission

Fifth Scene ....Same as Scene Two
Sixth Scene ....A Courtroom in the Beyond
Seventh Scene ....Before Julie's Door

Produced under the direction of FRANK REICHER
Costumes and scenery designed by LEE SIMONSON
Technical Director SHELDON K. VIELE
Scenery painted by ROBERT BERGMAN
Costumes executed by NETTIE DUFF READE
Stage Manager WALTER GEER
Assistant Stage Manager JACOB WEISER
Music arranged by DEEMS TAYLOR
Executive Director THERESA HELBURN

INTRODUCTION

The première of "LILIOM" at Budapest in December, 1909, left both playgoer and critic a bit bewildered. It was not the sort of play the Hungarian capital had been accustomed to expect of its favorite dramatist, whose THE DEVIL, after two years of unprecedented success, was still crowding the theatres of two continents.

One must, it was true, count on a touch of fantasy in every Molnar work. Never had he been wholly content with everyday reality, not in his stories, or in his sketches or in his earlier plays; and least of all in THE DEVIL wherein the natural and supernatural were most whimsically blended. But in LILIOM, it seemed, he had carried fantasy to quite unintelligible lengths. Budapest was frankly puzzled.

What did he mean by killing his hero in the fifth scene, taking him into Heaven in the sixth and bringing him back to earth in the seventh? Was this prosaic Heaven of his seriously or satirically intended? Was Liliom a saint or a common tough? And was his abortive redemption a symbol or merely

INTRODUCTION

a jibe? These were some of the questions Budapest debated while the play languished through thirty or forty performances and was withdrawn.

Almost ten years passed before it was revived. This time it was an immediate and overwhelming triumph. Perhaps the wide circulation of the play in printed form had made its beauty and significance clearer. Perhaps the tragedy of the war had made Molnar's public more sensitive to spiritual values. Whatever the reason, Budapest now accepted ecstatically what it had previously rejected, and Molnar was more of a popular hero than ever. From which it may be gleaned that Hungary takes its drama and dramatists more seriously, disapproves them more passionately and praises them more affectionately than we Americans can conceive. In Paris I once saw an audience rise en masse, because the sculptor Rodin had entered the auditorium, and remain on its feet cheering until he had taken his seat. Something of the kind greets Molnar whenever he appears in public, and nothing is more certain than that he is the hero, the oracle, the spoiled darling of club, salon and coffee house in which artistic Hungary foregathers.

But the years immediately following the first production of LILIOM were for him a period of eclipse. It was the first time that even the threat of failure had cast its shadow across his career. He became

INTRODUCTION

timid, wary of failure, too anxious to please his public. His subsequent plays were less original, less daring, more faithful to routine. Never again did he touch the heights of LILIOM; and some of his best friends aver that he never will again until he has banished the dread of failure that obsesses him.

An odd situation, truly, and in some aspects a tragic one. Genius lacking the courage to spread its wings and soar. A potential immortal bidding fearfully for the praise of a coffee-house clique. Is it vanity? Is it abnormal sensitiveness? Biographical data cast little light on the enigma.

Franz Molnar was born in Budapest on January 12, 1878, the son of a wealthy Jewish merchant. He graduated from the Universities of Geneva and Budapest. His literary career was begun as a journalist at the age of eighteen. He wrote short sketches and humorous dialogues of such beauty and charm that he became a national figure almost at once, and the circulation of his newspaper increased until it was foremost in Budapest. Then he married Margaret Vaszi, the daughter of his editor, herself a journalist of note. Two years later he was divorced from her, and subsequently he married an actress who had played rôles in his own plays.

For a portrait of him as he is today you have to think of Oscar Wilde at the height of his glory. A big pudgy face, immobile, pink, smooth-shaven,

INTRODUCTION

its child-like expressionlessness accentuated by the monocle he always wears, though rather belied by the gleam of humor in his dark alert eyes. His hair is iron-gray, his figure stocky and of about medium height. A mordant wit, an inimitable raconteur, he loves life and gayety and all the luxuries of life. Nothing can persuade him out of his complacent and comfortable routine. He will not leave Budapest, even to attend the première of one of his plays in nearby Vienna. The post-war political upheaval which has rent all Hungary into two voluble and bitter factions left him quite unperturbed and neutral. His pen is not for politics.

Yet it is a singularly prolific pen. His novels and short stories are among the finest in Hungarian literature. He has written nine long plays and numerous short ones. A chronology of his more important dramatic works is as follows:

1902 A DOKTOR UR (The Doctor).

1904 JOZSI.

1907 AZ ÖRDÖG (The Devil).

1909 LILIOM.

1911 TESTÖR (Played in this country as "Where Ignorance is Bliss").

1913 A FARKAS (Played in this country as "The Phantom Rival").

1914 URIDIVAT (Attorney for Defence).

1919 A HATTYU (The Swan).

INTRODUCTION

1920 SZINHAZ (Theatre: Three One-Act Plays).

Undoubtedly the greatest of these is LILIOM. Indeed, I know of no play written in our own time which matches the amazing virtuosity of LILIOM, its imaginative daring, its uncanny blending of naturalism and fantasy, humor and pathos, tenderness and tragedy into a solid dramatic structure. At first reading it may seem a mere improvization in many moods, but closer study must reveal how the moods are as inevitably related to each other as pearls on a string.

And where in modern dramatic literature can such pearls be matched—Julie incoherently confessing to her dead lover the love she had always been ashamed to tell; Liliom crying out to the distant carousel the glad news that he is to be a father; the two thieves gambling for the spoils of their prospective robbery; Marie and Wolf posing for their portrait while the broken-hearted Julie stands looking after the vanishing Liliom, the thieves' song ringing in her ears; the two policemen grousing about pay and pensions while Liliom lies bleeding to death; Liliom furtively proffering his daughter the star he has stolen for her in heaven. . . . The temptation to count the whole scintillating string is difficult to resist.

What is the moral of LILIOM? Nothing you can reduce to a creed. Molnar is not a preacher or a

INTRODUCTION

propagandist for any theory of life. You will look in vain in his plays for moral or dogma. His philosophy—if philosophy you can call it—is always implicit. And nothing is plainer than that his picture of a courtroom in the beyond is neither devoutly nor satirically intended. Liliom's Heaven is the Heaven of his own imagining. And what is more natural than that it should be an irrational jumble of priest's purgatory, police magistrate's justice and his own limited conception of good deeds and evil?

For those who hold that every fine dramatic architecture must have its spire of meaning, that by the very selection of character and incident the dramatist writes his commentary on life, there is still an explanation possible. Perhaps Molnar was at the old, old task of revaluing our ideas of good and evil. Perhaps he has only shown how the difference between a bully, a wife-beater and a criminal on the one hand and a saint on the other can be very slight. If one must tag LILIOM with a moral, I prefer to read mine in Liliom's dying speech to Julie wherein he says: "Nobody's right . . . but they all think they are right. . . . A lot they know."

BENJAMIN F. GLAZER.

New York, April, 1921.

LILIOM

SYNOPSIS OF SCENES

PROLOGUE—*An amusement park on the outskirts of Budapest.*

FIRST SCENE—*A lonely place in the park.*

SECOND SCENE—*The photographic studio of the* HOLLUNDERS.

THIRD SCENE—*Same as scene two.*

FOURTH SCENE—*A railroad embankment outside the city.*

FIFTH SCENE—*Same as scene two.*

SIXTH SCENE—*A courtroom in the beyond.*

SEVENTH SCENE—JULIE'S *garden.*

There are intermissions only after the second and fifth scenes.

CAST OF CHARACTERS

LILIOM ....
JULIE ....
MARIE ....
MRS. MUSKAT ....
LOUISE ....
MRS. HOLLUNDER ....
FICSUR ....
YOUNG HOLLUNDER ....
WOLF BEIFELD ....
THE CARPENTER ....
LINZMAN ....
THE DOCTOR ....
THE MAGISTRATE ....
TWO MOUNTED POLICEMEN ....
TWO PLAINCLOTHES POLICEMEN ....
TWO HEAVENLY POLICEMEN ....
THE RICHLY DRESSED MAN ....
THE POORLY DRESSED MAN ....
THE GUARD ....
A SUBURBAN POLICEMAN ....

THE PROLOGUE

An amusement park on the outskirts of Budapest on a late afternoon in Spring. Barkers stand before the booths of the sideshows haranguing the passing crowd. The strident music of a calliope is heard; laughter, shouts, the scuffle of feet, the signal bells of merry-go-round.

The merry-go-round is at Center. LILIOM stands at the entrance, a cigarette in his mouth, coaxing the people in. The girls regard him with idolizing glances and screech with pleasure as he playfully pushes them through entrance. Now and then some girl's escort resents the familiarity, whereupon LILIOM's demeanor becomes ugly and menacing, and the cowed escort slinks through the entrance behind his girl or contents himself with a muttered resentful comment.

One girl hands LILIOM a red carnation; he rewards her with a bow and a smile. When the soldier who accompanies her protests, LILIOM cows him with a fierce glance and a threatening gesture. MARIE and JULIE come out of the crowd and LILIOM favors them with particular notice as they pass into the merry-go-round.

Mrs. Muskat comes out of the merry-go-round, bringing Liliom coffee and rolls. Liliom mounts the barker's stand at the entrance, where he is elevated over everyone on the stage. Here he begins his harangue. Everybody turns toward him. The other booths are gradually deserted. The tumult makes it impossible for the audience to hear what he is saying, but every now and then some witticism of his provokes a storm of laughter which is audible above the din. Many people enter the merry-go-round. Here and there one catches a phrase "Room for one more on the zebra's back," "Which of you ladies?" "Ten heller for adults, five for children," "Step right up"——

It is growing darker. A lamplighter crosses the stage, and begins unperturbedly lighting the colored gas-lamps. The whistle of a distant locomotive is heard. Suddenly the tumult ceases, the lights go out, and the curtain falls in darkness.

END OF PROLOGUE

LILIOM

SCENE ONE

Scene—*A lonely place in the park, half hidden by trees and shrubbery. Under a flowering acacia tree stands a painted wooden bench. From the distance, faintly, comes the tumult of the amusement park. It is the sunset of the same day.*

When the curtain rises the stage is empty.

Marie *enters quickly, pauses at center, and looks back.*

MARIE

Julie, Julie! [*There is no answer.*] Do you hear me, Julie? Let her be! Come on. Let her be. [*Starts to go back.*]

[Julie *enters, looks back angrily.*]

JULIE

Did you ever hear of such a thing? What's the matter with the woman anyway?

MARIE

[*Looking back again.*] Here she comes again.

JULIE

Let her come. I didn't do anything to her. All of a sudden she comes up to me and begins to raise a row.

MARIE

Here she is. Come on, let's run. [*Tries to urge her off.*]

JULIE

Run? I should say not. What would I want to run for? I'm not afraid of her.

MARIE

Oh, come on. She'll only start a fight.

JULIE

I'm going to stay right here. Let her *start* a fight.

MRS. MUSKAT

[*Entering.*] What do you want to run away for? [*To Julie.*] Don't worry. I won't eat you. But there's one thing I want to tell you, my dear. Don't let me catch you in my carousel again. I stand for a whole lot, I have to in my business. It makes no difference to me whether my customers are ladies or the likes of you—as long as they pay their money. But when a girl misbehaves herself on my carousel—out she goes. Do you understand?

Julie

Are you talking to me?

Mrs. Muskat

Yes, you! You—chamber-maid, you! In my carousel——

Julie

Who did anything in your old carousel? I paid my fare and took my seat and never said a word, except to my friend here.

Marie

No, she never opened her mouth. Liliom came over to her of his own accord.

Mrs. Muskat

It's all the same. I'm not going to get in trouble with the police, and lose my license on account of you—you shabby kitchen maid!

Julie

Shabby yourself.

Mrs. Muskat

You stay out of my carousel! Letting my barker fool with you! Aren't you ashamed of yourself?

Julie

What? What did you say?

MRS. MUSKAT

I suppose you think I have no eyes in my head. I see everything that goes on in my carousel. During the whole ride she let Liliom fool with her—the shameless hussy!

JULIE

He did not fool with me! I don't let any man fool with me!

MRS. MUSKAT

He leaned against you all through the ride!

JULIE

He leaned against the panther. He always leans against something, doesn't he? Everybody leans where he wants. I couldn't tell him not to lean, if he always leans, could I? But he didn't lay a hand on me.

MRS. MUSKAT

Oh, didn't he? And I suppose he didn't put his hand around your waist, either?

MARIE

And if he did? What of it?

MRS. MUSKAT

You hold your tongue! No one's asking you—just you keep out of it.

JULIE

He put his arm around my waist—just the same as he does to all the girls. He always does that.

MRS. MUSKAT

I'll teach him not to do it any more, my dear. No carryings on in my carousel! If you are looking for that sort of thing, you'd better go to the circus! You'll find lots of soldiers there to carry on with!

JULIE

You keep your soldiers for yourself!

MARIE

Soldiers! As if we wanted soldiers!

MRS. MUSKAT

Well, I only want to tell you this, my dear, so that we understand each other perfectly. If you ever stick your nose in my carousel again, you'll wish you hadn't! I'm not going to lose my license on account of the likes of you! People who don't know how to behave, have got to stay out!

JULIE

You're wasting your breath. If I feel like riding on your carousel I'll pay my ten heller and I'll ride. I'd like to see anyone try to stop me!

Mrs. Muskat

Just come and try it, my dear—just come and try it.

Marie

We'll see what'll happen.

Mrs. Muskat

Yes, you will see something happen that never happened before in this park.

Julie

Perhaps you think you could throw me out!

Mrs. Muskat

I'm sure of it, my dear.

Julie

And suppose I'm stronger than you?

Mrs. Muskat

I'd think twice before I'd dirty my hands on a common servant girl. I'll have Liliom throw you out. He knows how to handle your kind.

Julie

You think Liliom would throw me out.

Mrs. Muskat

Yes, my dear, so fast that you won't know what happened to you!

Julie

He'd throw me—— [*Stops suddenly, for* Mrs. Muskat *has turned away. Both look off stage until* Liliom *enters, surrounded by four giggling servant girls.*]

Liliom

Go away! Stop following me, or I'll smack your face!

A Little Servant Girl

Well, give me back my handkerchief.

Liliom

Go on now——

The Four Servant Girls

[*Simultaneously.*] What do you think of him?—My handkerchief!—Give it back to her!—That's a nice thing to do!

The Little Servant Girl

[*To* Mrs. Muskat.] Please, lady, make him——

Mrs. Muskat

Oh, shut up!

Liliom

Will you get out of here? [*Makes a threatening gesture—the four servant girls exit in voluble but fearful haste.*]

Mrs. Muskat

What have you been doing now?

Liliom

None of your business. [*Glances at* Julie.] Have you been starting with her again?

Julie

Mister Liliom, please——

Liliom

[*Steps threateningly toward her.*] Don't yell!

Julie

[*Timidly.*] I didn't yell.

Liliom

Well, don't. [*To* Mrs. Muskat.] What's the matter? What has she done to you?

Mrs. Muskat

What has she done? She's been impudent to me. Just as impudent as she could be! I put her out of the carousel. Take a good look at this innocent thing, Liliom. She's never to be allowed in my carousel again!

Liliom

[*To* Julie.] You heard that. Run home, now.

Marie

Come on. Don't waste your time with such people. [*Tries to lead* Julie *away.*]

Julie

No, I won't——

Mrs. Muskat

If she ever comes again, you're not to let her in. And if she gets in before you see her, throw her out. Understand?

Liliom

What has she done, anyhow?

Julie

[*Agitated and very earnest.*] Mister Liliom—tell me please—honest and truly—if I come into the carousel, will you throw me out?

Mrs. Muskat

Of course he'll throw you out.

Marie

She wasn't talking to you.

Julie

Tell me straight to my face, Mister Liliom, would you throw me out? [*They face each other. There is a brief pause.*]

LILIOM

Yes, little girl, if there was a reason—but if there was no reason, why should I throw you out?

MARIE

[*To* MRS. MUSKAT.] There, you see!

JULIE

Thank you, Mister Liliom.

MRS. MUSKAT

And I tell you again, if this little slut dares to set her foot in my carousel, she's to be thrown out! I'll stand for no indecency in my establishment.

LILIOM

What do you mean—indecency?

MRS. MUSKAT

I saw it all. There's no use denying it.

JULIE

She says you put your arm around my waist.

LILIOM

Me?

MRS. MUSKAT

Yes, you! I saw you. Don't play the innocent.

Liliom

Here's something new! I'm not to put my arm around a girl's waist any more! I suppose I'm to ask your permission before I touch another girl!

Mrs. Muskat

You can touch as many girls as you want and as often as you want—for my part you can go as far as you like with any of them—but not this one—I permit no indecency in my carousel. [*There is a long pause.*]

Liliom

[*To* Mrs. Muskat.] And now I'll ask you please to shut your mouth.

Mrs. Muskat

What?

Liliom

Shut your mouth quick, and go back to your carousel.

Mrs. Muskat

What?

Liliom

What did she do to you, anyhow? Tryin' to start a fight with a little pigeon like that . . . just because I touched her?—You come to the carousel as often as you want to, little girl. Come every afternoon, and sit on the panther's back, and if you haven't got the price, Liliom will pay for you. And if anyone dares to bother you, you come and tell *me*.

MRS. MUSKAT

You reprobate!

LILIOM

Old witch!

JULIE

Thank you, Mister Liliom.

MRS. MUSKAT

You seem to think that I can't throw you out, too. What's the reason I can't? Because you are the best barker in the park? Well, you are very much mistaken. In fact, you can consider yourself thrown out already. You're discharged!

LILIOM

Very good.

MRS. MUSKAT

[*Weakening a little.*] I can discharge you any time I feel like it.

LILIOM

Very good, you feel like discharging me. I'm discharged. That settles it.

MRS. MUSKAT

Playing the high and mighty, are you? Conceited pig! Good-for-nothing!

Liliom

You said you'd throw me out, didn't you? Well, that suits me; I'm thrown out.

Mrs. Muskat

[*Softening.*] Do you have to take up every word I say?

Liliom

It's all right; it's all settled. I'm a good-for-nothing. And a conceited pig. And I'm discharged.

Mrs. Muskat

Do you want to ruin my business?

Liliom

A good-for-nothing? Now I know! And I'm discharged! Very good.

Mrs. Muskat

You're a devil, you are . . . and that woman——

Liliom

Keep away from her!

Mrs. Muskat

I'll get Hollinger to give you such a beating that you'll hear all the angels sing . . . and it won't be the first time, either.

LILIOM

Get out of here. I'm discharged. And you get out of here.

JULIE

[*Timidly.*] Mister Liliom, if she's willing to say that she hasn't discharged you——

LILIOM

You keep out of this.

JULIE

[*Timidly.*] I don't want this to happen on account of me.

LILIOM

[*To* MRS. MUSKAT, *pointing to* JULIE.] Apologize to her!

MARIE

A-ha!

MRS. MUSKAT

Apologize? To who?

LILIOM

To this little pigeon. Well—are you going to do it?

MRS. MUSKAT

If you give me this whole park on a silver plate, and all the gold of the Rothschilds on top of it— I'd—I'd—— Let her dare to come into my carousel again and she'll get thrown out so hard that she'll see stars in daylight!

Liliom

In that case, dear lady [*takes off his cap with a flourish*], you are respectfully requested to get out o' here as fast as your legs will carry you—I never beat up a woman yet—except that Holzer woman who I sent to the hospital for three weeks—but—if you don't get out o' here this minute, and let this little squab be, I'll give you the prettiest slap in the jaw you ever had in your life.

Mrs. Muskat

Very good, my son. Now you *can* go to the devil. Good-bye. You're discharged, and you needn't try to come back, either. [*She exits. It is beginning to grow dark.*]

Marie

[*With grave concern.*] Mister Liliom——

Liliom

Don't you pity me or I'll give *you* a slap in the jaw. [*To* Julie.] And don't you pity me, either.

Julie

[*In alarm.*] I don't pity you, Mister Liliom.

Liliom

You're a liar, you *are* pitying me. I can see it in your face. You're thinking, now that Madame Muskat has thrown him out, Liliom will have to go begging. Huh! Look at me. I'm big enough to get along without a Madame Muskat. I have been thrown out of better jobs than hers.

JULIE

What will you do now, Mister Liliom?

LILIOM

Now? First of all, I'll go and get myself—a glass of beer. You see, when something happens to annoy me, I always drink a glass of beer.

JULIE

Then you *are* annoyed about losing your job.

LILIOM

No, only about where I'm going to get the beer.

MARIE

Well—eh——

LILIOM

Well—eh—what?

MARIE

Well—eh—are you going to stay with us, Mister Liliom?

LILIOM

Will you pay for the beer? [MARIE *looks doubtful; he turns to* JULIE.] Will you? [*She does not answer.*] How much money have you got?

JULIE

[*Bashfully.*] Eight heller.

LILIOM

And you? [MARIE *casts down her eyes and does not reply.* LILIOM *continues sternly.*] I asked you how much you've got? [MARIE *begins to weep softly.*] I understand. Well, you needn't cry about it. You girls stay here, while I go back to the carousel and get my clothes and things. And when I come back, we'll go to the Hungarian beer-garden. It's all right, I'll pay. Keep your money. [*He exits.* MARIE *and* JULIE *stand silent, watching him until he has gone.*]

MARIE

Are you sorry for him?

JULIE

Are you?

MARIE

Yes, a little. Why are you looking after him in that funny way?

JULIE

[*Sits down.*] Nothing—except I'm sorry he lost his job.

MARIE

[*With a touch of pride.*] It was on our account he lost his job. Because he's fallen in love with you.

JULIE

He hasn't at all.

MARIE

[*Confidently.*] Oh, yes! he is in love with you. [*Hesitantly, romantically.*] There is someone in love with me, too.

JULIE

There is? Who?

MARIE

I—I never mentioned it before, because you hadn't a lover of your own—but now you have—and I'm free to speak. [*Very grandiloquently.*] My heart has found its mate.

JULIE

You're only making it up.

MARIE

No, it's true—my heart's true love——

JULIE

Who? Who is he?

MARIE

A soldier.

JULIE

What kind of a soldier?

MARIE

I don't know. Just a soldier. Are there different kinds?

JULIE

Many different kinds. There are hussars, artillerymen, engineers, infantry—that's the kind that walks—and——

MARIE

How can you tell which is which?

JULIE

By their uniforms.

MARIE

[*After trying to puzzle it out.*] The conductors on the street cars—are they soldiers?

JULIE

Certainly not. They're conductors.

MARIE

Well, they have uniforms.

JULIE

But they don't carry swords or guns.

MARIE

Oh! [*Thinks it over again; then.*] Well, policemen—are they?

JULIE

[*With a touch of exasperation.*] Are they what?

MARIE
Soldiers.

JULIE
Certainly not. They're just policemen.

MARIE
[*Triumphantly.*] But they have uniforms—and they carry weapons, too.

JULIE
You're just as dumb as you can be. You don't go by their uniforms.

MARIE
But you said——

JULIE
No, I didn't. A letter-carrier wears a uniform, too, but that doesn't make him a soldier.

MARIE
But if he carried a gun or a sword, would he be——

JULIE
No, he'd still be a letter-carrier. You can't go by guns or swords, either.

MARIE
Well, if you don't go by the uniforms or the weapons, what *do* you go by?

JULIE

By——— [*Tries to put it into words; fails; then breaks off suddenly.*] Oh, you'll get to know when you've lived in the city long enough. You're nothing but a country girl. When you've lived in the city a year, like I have, you'll know all about it.

MARIE

[*Half angrily.*] Well, how *do* you know when *you* see a real soldier?

JULIE

By one thing.

MARIE

What?

JULIE

One thing——— [*She pauses.* MARIE *starts to cry.*] Oh, what are you crying about?

MARIE

Because you're making fun of me. . . . You're a city girl, and I'm just fresh from the country . . . and how am I expected to know a soldier when I see one? . . . You, you ought to tell me, instead of making fun of me———

JULIE

All right. Listen then, cry-baby. There's only one way to tell a soldier: by his salute! That's the only way.

MARIE

[*Joyfully; with a sigh of relief.*] Ah—that's good.

JULIE

What?

MARIE

I say—it's all right then—because Wolf—Wolf—— [JULIE *laughs derisively.*] Wolf—that's his name. [*She weeps again.*]

JULIE

Crying again? What now?

MARIE

You're making fun of me again.

JULIE

I'm not. But when you say, "Wolf—Wolf—" like that, I have to laugh, don't I? [*Archly.*] What's his name again?

MARIE

I won't tell you.

JULIE

All right. If you won't say it, then he's no soldier.

MARIE

I'll say it.

JULIE
Go on.

MARIE
No, I won't. [*She weeps again.*]

JULIE
Then he's not a soldier. I guess he's a letter-carrier——

MARIE
No—no—I'd rather say it.

JULIE
Well, then.

MARIE
[*Giggling.*] But you mustn't look at me. You look the other way, and I'll say it. [JULIE *looks away.* MARIE *can hardly restrain her own laughter.*] Wolf! [*She laughs.*] That's his real name. Wolf, Wolf, Soldier—Wolf!

JULIE
What kind of a uniform does he wear?

MARIE
Red.

JULIE
Red trousers?

MARIE
No.

JULIE

Red coat?

MARIE

No.

JULIE

What then?

MARIE

[*Triumphantly.*] His cap!

JULIE

[*After a long pause.*] He's just a porter, you dunce. Red cap . . . that's a porter—and he doesn't carry a gun or a sword, either.

MARIE

[*Triumphantly.*] But he salutes. You said yourself that was the only way to tell a soldier——

JULIE

He doesn't salute at all. He only greets people——

MARIE

He salutes me. . . . And if his name *is* Wolf, that doesn't prove he ain't a soldier—he salutes, and he wears a red cap and he stands on guard all day long outside a big building——

JULIE

What does he do there?

MARIE

[*Seriously.*] He spits.

JULIE

[*With contempt.*] He's nothing—nothing but a common porter.

MARIE

What's Liliom?

JULIE

[*Indignantly.*] Why speak of him? What has he to do with me?

MARIE

The same as Wolf has to do with me. If you can talk to me like that about Wolf, I can talk to you about Liliom.

JULIE

He's nothing to me. He put his arm around me in the carousel. I couldn't tell him not to put his arm around me after he had done it, could I?

MARIE

I suppose you didn't like him to do it?

JULIE

No.

MARIE

Then why are you waiting for him? Why don't you *go* home?

JULIE

Why—eh—he *said* we were to wait for him.
[LILIOM *enters. There is a long silence.*]

LILIOM

Are you still here? What are you waiting for?

MARIE

You told us to wait.

LILIOM

Must you always interfere? No one is talking to you.

MARIE

You asked us—why we——

LILIOM

Will you keep your mouth shut? What do you suppose I want with two of you? I meant that one of you was to wait. The other can go home.

MARIE

All right.

JULIE

All right. [*Neither starts to go.*]

LILIOM

One of you goes home. [*To* MARIE.] Where do you work?

MARIE

At the Breier's, Damjanovitsch Street, Number 20.

LILIOM

And you?

JULIE

I work there, too.

LILIOM

Well, one of you goes home. Which of you wants to stay. [*There is no answer.*] Come on, speak up, which of you stays?

MARIE

[*Officiously.*] She'll lose her job if she stays.

LILIOM

Who will?

MARIE

Julie. She has to be back by seven o'clock.

LILIOM

Is that true? Will they discharge you if you're not back on time?

JULIE

Yes.

LILIOM

Well, wasn't I discharged?

JULIE

Yes—you were discharged, too.

Marie

Julie, shall I go?

Julie

I—can't tell you what to do.

Marie

All right—stay if you like.

Liliom

You'll be discharged if you do?

Marie

Shall I go, Julie?

Julie

[*Embarrassed.*] Why do you keep asking me that?

Marie

You know best what to do.

Julie

[*Profoundly moved; slowly.*] It's all right, Marie, you can go home.

Marie

[*Exits reluctantly, but comes back, and says uncertainly.*] Good-night. [*She waits a moment to see if* Julie *will follow her.* Julie *does not move.* Marie *exits. Meantime it has grown quite dark. During the following scene the gas-lamps far in the distance are lighted one by one. LILIOM and JULIE sit on the bench. From afar, very faintly, comes the music of a calliope. But the music is intermittently heard; now it breaks off, now it resumes again, as if it came down on a fitful wind. Blending with it are the sounds of human voices, now loud, now soft; the blare of a toy trumpet; the confused noises of the show-booths. It grows progressively darker until the end of the scene. There is no moonlight. The spring irridescence glows in the deep blue sky.]*

LILIOM

Now we're both discharged. [*She does not answer. From now on they speak gradually lower and lower until the end of the scene, which is played almost in whispers. Whistles softly, then.*] Have you had your supper?

JULIE

No.

LILIOM

Want to go eat something at the Garden?

JULIE

No.

LILIOM

Anywhere else?

JULIE

No.

Liliom

[*Whistles softly, then.*] You don't come to this park very often, do you? I've only seen you three times. Been here oftener than that?

Julie

Oh, yes.

Liliom

Did you see me?

Julie

Yes.

Liliom

And did you know I was Liliom?

Julie

They told me.

Liliom

[*Whistles softly, then.*] Have you got a sweetheart?

Julie

No.

Liliom

Don't lie to me.

Julie

I haven't. If I had, I'd tell you. I've never had one.

Liliom

What an awful liar you are. I've got a good mind to go away and leave you here.

JULIE

I've never had one.

LILIOM

Tell that to someone else.

JULIE

[*Reproachfully.*] Why do you insist I have?

LILIOM

Because you stayed here with me the first time I asked you to. You know your way around, you do.

JULIE

No, I don't, Mister Liliom.

LILIOM

I suppose you'll tell me you don't know why you're sitting here—like this, in the dark, alone with me—You wouldn't 'a' stayed so quick, if you hadn't done it before—with some soldier, maybe. This isn't the first time. You wouldn't have been so ready to stay if it was—what *did* you stay for, anyhow?

JULIE

So you wouldn't be left alone.

LILIOM

Alone! God, you're dumb! I don't need to be alone. I can have all the girls I want. Not only servant girls like you, but cooks and governesses, even French girls. I could have twenty of them if I wanted to.

Julie

I know, Mister Liliom.

Liliom

What do you know?

Julie

That all the girls are in love with you. But that's not why *I* stayed. I stayed because you've been so good to me.

Liliom

Well, then you can go home.

Julie

I don't want to go home now.

Liliom

And what if I go away and leave you sitting here?

Julie

If you did, I wouldn't go home.

Liliom

Do you know what you remind me of? A sweetheart I had once—I'll tell you how I met her—— One night, at closing time, we had put out the lights in the carousel, and just as I was—— [*He is in-*

terrupted by the entrance of two plainclothes policemen. They take their stations on either side of the bench. They are police, searching the park for vagabonds.]

FIRST POLICEMAN

What are you doing there?

LILIOM

Me?

SECOND POLICEMAN

Stand up when you're spoken to! [*He taps* LILIOM *imperatively on the shoulder.*]

FIRST POLICEMAN

What's your name?

LILIOM

Andreas Zavoczki. [JULIE *begins to weep softly.*]

SECOND POLICEMAN

Stop your bawling. We're not goin' to eat you. We are only making our rounds.

FIRST POLICEMAN

See that he doesn't get away. [THE SECOND POLICEMAN *steps closer to* LILIOM.] What's your business?

LILIOM

Barker and bouncer.

Second Policeman

They call him Liliom, Chief. We've had him up a couple of times.

First Policeman

So that's who you are! Who do you work for now?

Liliom

I work for the widow Muskat.

First Policeman

What are you hanging around here for?

Liliom

We're just sitting here—me and this girl.

First Policeman

Your sweetheart?

Liliom

No.

First Policeman

[*To* Julie.] And who are you?

Julie

Julie Zeller.

First Policeman

Servant girl?

JULIE

Maid of All Work for Mister Georg Breier, Number Twenty Damjanovitsch Street.

FIRST POLICEMAN

Show your hands.

SECOND POLICEMAN

[*After examining* JULIE's *hand.*] Servant girl.

FIRST POLICEMAN

Why aren't you at home? What are you doing out here with him?

JULIE

This is my day out, sir.

FIRST POLICEMAN

It would be better for you if you didn't spend it sitting around with a fellow like this.

SECOND POLICEMAN

They'll be disappearing in the bushes as soon as we turn our backs.

FIRST POLICEMAN

He's only after your money. We know this fine fellow. He picks up you silly servant girls and takes what money you have. Tomorrow you'll probably be coming around to report him. If you do, I'll throw you out.

Julie

I haven't any money, sir.

First Policeman

Do you hear that, Liliom?

Liliom

I'm not looking for her money.

Second Policeman

[*Nudging him warningly.*] Keep your mouth shut.

First Policeman

It is my duty to warn you, my child, what kind of company you're in. He makes a specialty of servant girls. That's why he works in a carousel. He gets hold of a girl, promises to marry her, then he takes her money and her ring.

Julie

But I haven't got a ring.

Second Policeman

You're not to talk unless you're asked a question.

First Policeman

You be thankful that I'm warning you. It's nothing to me what you do. I'm not your father, thank God. But I'm telling you what kind of a fellow he is. By tomorrow morning you'll be coming around to us to report him. Now you be sensible and go home. You needn't be afraid of him. This officer will take you home if you're afraid.

Julie
Do I *have* to go?

First Policeman
No, you don't *have* to go.

Julie
Then I'll stay, sir.

First Policeman
Well, you've been warned.

Julie
Yes, sir. Thank you, sir.

First Policeman
Come on, Berkovics. [*The* Policemen *exit.* Julie *and* Liliom *sit on the bench again. There is a brief pause.*]

Julie
Well, and what then?

Liliom
[*Fails to understand.*] Huh?

JULIE

You were beginning to tell me a story.

LILIOM

Me?

JULIE

Yes, about a sweetheart. You said, one night, just as they were putting out the lights of the carousel—— That's as far as you got.

LILIOM

Oh, yes, yes, just as the lights were going out, someone came along—a little girl with a big shawl—you know—— She came—eh—from—— Say—tell me—ain't you—that is, ain't you at all—afraid of me? The officer told you what kind of a fellow I am—and that I'd take your money away from you——

JULIE

You couldn't take it away—I haven't got any. But if I had—I'd—I'd give it to you—I'd give it all to you.

LILIOM

You would?

JULIE

If you asked me for it.

LILIOM

Have you ever had a fellow you gave money to?

JULIE
No.

LILIOM
Haven't you ever had a sweetheart?

JULIE
No.

LILIOM
Someone you used to go walking with. You've had one like that?

JULIE
Yes.

LILIOM
A soldier?

JULIE
He came from the same village I did.

LILIOM
That's what all the soldiers say. Where *do* you come from, anyway?

JULIE
Not far from here. [*There is a pause.*]

LILIOM
Were you in love with him?

JULIE
Why do you keep asking me that all the time, Mister Liliom? I wasn't in love with him. We only went walking together.

LILIOM
Where did you walk?

JULIE
In the park.

LILIOM
And your virtue? Where did you lose that?

JULIE
I haven't got any virtue.

LILIOM
Well, you had once.

JULIE
No, I never had. I'm a respectable girl.

LILIOM
Yes, but you gave the soldier something.

JULIE
Why do you question me like that, Mister Liliom?

LILIOM
Did you give him something?

JULIE
You have to. But I didn't love him.

LILIOM
Do you love me?

JULIE

No, Mister Liliom.

LILIOM

Then why do you stay here with me?

JULIE

Um—nothing. [*There is a pause. The music from afar is plainly heard.*]

LILIOM

Want to dance?

JULIE

No. I have to be very careful.

LILIOM

Of what?

JULIE

My—character.

LILIOM

Why?

JULIE

Because I'm never going to marry. If I was going to marry, it would be different. Then I wouldn't need to worry so much about my character. It doesn't make any difference if you're married. But I shan't marry—and that's why I've got to take care to be a respectable girl.

LILIOM

Suppose I were to say to you—I'll marry you.

JULIE

You?

LILIOM

That frightens you, doesn't it? You're thinking of what the officer said and you're afraid.

JULIE

No, I'm not, Mister Liliom. I don't pay any attention to what he said.

LILIOM

But you wouldn't dare to marry anyone like me, would you?

JULIE

I know that—that—if I loved anyone—it wouldn't make any difference to me what he—even if I died for it.

LILIOM

But you wouldn't marry a rough guy like me—that is,—eh—if you loved me——

JULIE

Yes, I would—if I loved you, Mister Liliom. [*There is a pause.*]

LILIOM

[*Whispers.*] Well,—you just said—didn't you?—that you don't love me. Well, why don't you go home then?

JULIE

It's too late now, they'd all be asleep.

LILIOM

Locked out?

JULIE

Certainly. [*They are silent a while.*]

LILIOM

I think—that even a low-down good-for-nothing—can make a man of himself.

JULIE

Certainly. [*They are silent again. A lamplighter crosses the stage, lights the lamp over the bench, and exits.*]

LILIOM

Are you hungry?

JULIE

No. [*Another pause.*]

LILIOM

Suppose—you had some money—and I took it from you?

JULIE

Then you could take it, that's all.

LILIOM

[*After another brief silence.*] All I have to do—is go back to her—that Muskat woman—she'll be glad to get me back—then I'd be earning my wages again. [*She is silent. The twilight folds darker about them.*]

JULIE

[*Very softly.*] Don't go back—to her—— [*Pause.*]

LILIOM

There are a lot of acacia trees around here. [*Pause.*]

JULIE

Don't go back to her—— [*Pause.*]

LILIOM

She'd take me back the minute I asked her. I know why—she knows, too—— [*Pause.*]

JULIE

I can smell them, too—acacia blossoms—— [*There is a pause. Some blossoms drift down from the tree-top to the bench.* LILIOM *picks one up and smells it.*]

LILIOM

White acacias!

JULIE

[*After a brief pause.*] The wind brings them down. [*They are silent. There is a long pause before*]

THE CURTAIN FALLS

SCENE TWO

Scene—*A photographer's "studio," operated by the* Hollunders, *on the fringe of the park. It is a dilapidated hovel. The general entrance is Back Left. Back Right there is a window with a sofa before it. The outlook is on the amusement park with perhaps a small Ferris-wheel or the scaffolding of a "scenic-railway" in the background.*

The door to the kitchen is up Left and a black-curtained entrance to the dark-room is down Left. Just in front of the dark room stands the camera on its tripod. Against the back wall, between the door and window, stands the inevitable photographer's background-screen, ready to be wheeled into place.

It is forenoon. When the curtain rises, Marie *and* Julie *are discovered.*

Marie

And *he* beat up Hollinger?

Julie

Yes, he gave him an awful licking.

Marie

But Hollinger is bigger than he is.

Julie

He licked him just the same. It isn't size that counts, you know, it's cleverness. And Liliom's awful quick.

Marie

And then he was arrested?

Julie

Yes, they arrested him, but they let him go the next day. That makes twice in the two months we've been living here that Liliom's been arrested and let go again.

Marie

Why do they let him go?

Julie

Because he is innocent.

[Mother Hollunder, *a very old woman, sharp-tongued, but in reality quite warm-hearted beneath her formidable exterior, enters at back carrying a few sticks of firewood, and scolding, half to herself.*]

Mother Hollunder

Always wanting something, but never willing to work for it. He won't work, and he won't steal, but he'll use up a poor old widow's last bit of firewood. He'll do that cheerfully enough! A big, strong lout like that lying around all day resting his lazy bones! He ought to be ashamed to look decent people in the face.

JULIE

I'm sorry, Mother Hollunder. . . .

MOTHER HOLLUNDER

Sorry! Better be sorry the lazy good-for-nothing ain't in jail where he belongs instead of in the way of honest, hard-working people. [*She exits into the kitchen.*]

MARIE

Who's that?

JULIE

Mrs. Hollunder—my aunt. This is her [*with a sweeping gesture that takes in the camera, darkroom and screen*] studio. She lets us live here for nothing.

MARIE

What's she fetching the wood for?

JULIE

She brings us everything we need. If it weren't for her I don't know what would become of us. She's a good-hearted soul even if her tongue is sharp. [*There is a pause.*]

MARIE

[*Shyly.*] Do you know—I've found out. He's not a soldier.

JULIE

Do you still see him?

MARIE

Oh, yes.

JULIE

Often?

MARIE

Very often. He's asked me——

JULIE

To marry you?

MARIE

To marry me.

JULIE

You see—that proves he isn't a soldier. [*There is another pause.*]

MARIE

[*Abashed, yet a bit boastfully.*] Do you know what I'm doing—I'm flirting with him.

JULIE

Flirting?

MARIE

Yes. He asks me to go to the park—and I say I can't go. Then he coaxes me, and promises me a new scarf for my head if I go. But I don't go —even then. . . . So then he walks all the way home with me—and I bid him good-night at the door.

JULIE

Is that what you call flirting?

MARIE

Um-hm! It's sinful, but it's so *thrilling*.

JULIE

Do you ever quarrel?

MARIE

[*Grandly.*] Only when our Passionate Love surges up.

JULIE

Your passionate love?

MARIE

Yes. . . . He takes my hand and we walk along together. Then he wants to swing hands, but I won't let him. I say: "Don't swing my hand"; and he says, "Don't be so stubborn." And then he tries to swing my hand again, but still I don't let him. And for a long time I don't let him—until in the end I let him. Then we walk along swinging hands—up and down, up and down—just like this. *That* is Passionate Love. It's sinful, but it's awfully *thrilling*.

Julie

You're happy, aren't you?

Marie

Happier than—anything—— But the most beautiful thing on earth is Ideal Love.

Julie

What kind is that?

Marie

Daylight comes about three in the morning this time of the year. When we've been up that long we're all through with flirting and Passionate Love—and then our Ideal Love comes to the surface. It comes like this: I'll be sitting on the bench and Wolf, he holds my hand tight—and he puts his cheek against my cheek and we don't talk . . . we just sit there very quiet. . . . And after a while he gets sleepy, and his head sinks down, and he falls asleep . . . but even in his sleep he holds tight to my hand. And I—I sit perfectly still just looking around me and taking long, deep breaths—for by that time it's morning and the trees and flowers are fresh with dew. But Wolf doesn't smell anything because he's so fast asleep. And I get awfully sleepy myself, but I don't sleep. And we sit like that for a long time. That is Ideal Love——
[*There is a long pause.*]

JULIE

[*Regretfully; uneasily.*] He went out last night and he hasn't come home yet.

MARIE

Here are sixteen Kreuzer. It was supposed to be carfare to take my young lady to the conservatory—eight there and eight back—but I made her walk. Here—save it with the rest.

JULIE

This makes three gulden, forty-six.

MARIE

Three gulden, forty-six.

JULIE

He won't work at all.

MARIE

Too lazy?

JULIE

No. He never learned a trade, you see, and he can't just go and be a day-laborer—so he just does nothing.

MARIE

That ain't right.

JULIE

No. Have the Breiers got a new maid yet?

MARIE

They've had three since you left. You know, Wolf's going to take a new job. He's going to work for the city. He'll get rent free, too.

JULIE

He won't go back to work at the carousel either. I ask him why, but he won't tell me—— Last Monday he hit me.

MARIE

Did you hit him back?

JULIE

No.

MARIE

Why don't you leave him?

JULIE

I don't want to.

MARIE

I would. I'd leave him. [*There is a strained silence.*]

MOTHER HOLLUNDER

[*Enters, carrying a pot of water; muttering aloud.*] He can play cards, all right. He can fight, too; and take money from poor servant girls. And the police turn their heads the other way—— The carpenter was here.

JULIE

Is that water for the soup?

MOTHER HOLLUNDER

The carpenter was here. There's a *man* for you! Dark, handsome, lots of hair, a respectable widower with two children—and money, and a good paying business.

JULIE

[*To* MARIE.] It's three gulden sixty-six, not forty-six.

MARIE

Yes, that's what I make it—sixty-six.

MOTHER HOLLUNDER

He wants to take her out of this and marry her. This is the fifth time he's been here. He has two children, but——

JULIE

Please don't bother, Aunt Hollunder, I'll get the water myself.

MOTHER HOLLUNDER

He's waiting outside now.

JULIE

Send him away.

Mother Hollunder

He'll only come back again—and first thing you know that vagabond will get jealous and there'll be a fight. [*Goes out, muttering.*] Oh, he's ready enough to fight, he is. Strike a poor little girl like that! Ought to be ashamed of himself! And the police just let him go on doing as he pleases. [*Still scolding, she exits at back.*]

Marie

A carpenter wants to marry you?

Julie

Yes.

Marie

Why don't you?

Julie

Because——

Marie

Liliom doesn't support you, and he beats you—he thinks he can do whatever he likes just because he's Liliom. He's a bad one.

Julie

He's not really bad.

Marie

That night you sat on the bench together—he was gentle then.

JULIE

Yes, he was gentle.

MARIE

And afterwards he got wild again.

JULIE

Afterwards he got wild—sometimes. But that night on the bench . . . he was gentle. He's gentle now, sometimes, very gentle. After supper, when he stands there and listens to the music of the carousel, something comes over him—and he is gentle.

MARIE

Does he say anything?

JULIE

He doesn't say anything. He gets thoughtful and very quiet, and his big eyes stare straight ahead of him.

MARIE

Into your eyes?

JULIE

Not exactly. He's unhappy because he isn't working. That's really why he hit me on Monday.

MARIE

That's a fine reason for hitting you! Beats his wife because he isn't working, the ruffian!

JULIE

It preys on his mind——

MARIE

Did he hurt you?

JULIE

[*Very eagerly.*] Oh, no.

MRS. MUSKAT

[*Enters haughtily.*] Good morning. Is Liliom home?

JULIE

No.

MRS. MUSKAT

Gone out?

JULIE

He hasn't come home yet.

MRS. MUSKAT

I'll wait for him. [*She sits down.*]

MARIE

You've got a lot of gall—to come here.

MRS. MUSKAT

Are you the lady of the house, my dear? Better look out or you'll get a slap in the mouth.

MARIE

How dare you set foot in Julie's house?

MRS. MUSKAT

[*To* JULIE.] Pay no attention to her, my child. You know what brings me here. That vagabond, that good-for-nothing, I've come to give him his bread and butter back.

MARIE

He's not dependent on you for his bread.

MRS. MUSKAT

[*To* JULIE.] Just ignore her, my child. She's just ignorant.

MARIE

[*Going.*] Good-bye.

JULIE

Good-bye.

MARIE

[*In the doorway, calling back.*] Sixty-six.

JULIE

Yes, sixty-six.

MARIE

Good-bye. [*She exits.* JULIE *starts to go toward the kitchen.*]

MRS. MUSKAT

I paid him a krone a day, and on Sunday a gulden. And he got all the beer and cigars he wanted from the customers. [JULIE *pauses on the threshold, but does not answer.*] And he'd rather starve than beg my pardon. Well, I don't insist on that. I'll take him back without it. [JULIE *does not answer.*] The fact is the people ask for him—and, you see, I've got to consider business first. It's nothing to me if he starves. I wouldn't be here at all, if it wasn't for business—— [*She pauses, for* LILIOM *and* FICSUR *have entered.*]

JULIE

Mrs. Muskat is here.

LILIOM

I see she is.

JULIE

You might say good-morning.

LILIOM

What for? And what do *you* want, anyhow?

JULIE

I don't want anything.

LILIOM

Then keep your mouth shut. Next thing you'll be starting to nag again about my being out all night and out of work and living on your relations——

JULIE

I'm not saying anything.

LILIOM

But it's all on the tip of your tongue—I know you—now don't start or you'll get another. [*He paces angrily up and down. They are all a bit afraid of him, and shrink and look away as he passes them. Ficsur shambles from place to place, his eyes cast down as if he were searching for something on the floor.*]

MRS. MUSKAT

[*Suddenly, to* FICSUR.] You're always dragging him out to play cards and drink with you. I'll have you locked up, I will.

FICSUR

I don't want to talk to you. You're too common. [*He goes out by the door at back and lingers there in plain view. There is a pause.*]

JULIE

Mrs. Muskat is here.

LILIOM

Well, why doesn't she open her mouth, if she has anything to say?

MRS. MUSKAT

Why do you go around with this man Ficsur? He'll get you mixed up in one of his robberies first thing you know.

LILIOM

What's it to you who I go with? I do what I please. What do you want?

MRS. MUSKAT

You know what I want.

LILIOM

No, I don't.

MRS. MUSKAT

What do you suppose I want? Think I've come just to pay a social call?

LILIOM

Do I owe you anything?

MRS. MUSKAT

Yes, you do—but that's not what I came for. You're a fine one to come to for money! You earn so much these days! You know very well what I'm here for.

LILIOM

You've got Hollinger at the carousel, haven't you?

MRS. MUSKAT

Sure I have.

LILIOM

Well, what else do you want? **He's as good** as I am.

MRS. MUSKAT

You're quite right, my boy. He's every bit as good as you are. I'd not dream of letting him go. But one isn't enough any more. There's work enough for two——

LILIOM

One was enough when *I* was there.

MRS. MUSKAT

Well, I might let Hollinger go——

LILIOM

Why let him go, if he's so good?

MRS. MUSKAT

[*Shrugs her shoulders.*] Yes, he's good. [*Not once until now has she looked at* LILIOM.]

LILIOM

[*To* JULIE.] Ask your aunt if I can have a cup of coffee. [JULIE *exits into the kitchen.*] So Hollinger is good, is he?

MRS. MUSKAT

[*Crosses to him and looks him in the face.*] Why don't you stay home and sleep at night? You're a sight to look at.

LILIOM

He's good, is he?

MRS. MUSKAT

Push your hair back from your forehead.

LILIOM

Let my hair be. It's nothing to you.

MRS. MUSKAT

All right. But if I'd told you to let it hang down over your eyes you'd have pushed it back—I hear you've been beating her, this—this——

LILIOM

None of your business.

MRS. MUSKAT

You're a fine fellow! Beating a skinny little thing like that! If you're tired of her, leave her, but there's no use beating the poor——

LILIOM

Leave her, eh? You'd like that, wouldn't you?

Mrs. Muskat

Don't flatter yourself. [*Quite embarrassed.*] Serves me right, too. If I had any sense I wouldn't have run after you—— My God, the things one must do for the sake of business! If I could only sell the carousel I wouldn't be sitting here. . . . Come, Liliom, if you have any sense, you'll come back. I'll pay you well.

Liliom

The carousel is crowded just the same . . . *without me?*

Mrs. Muskat

Crowded, yes—but it's not the same.

Liliom

Then you admit that you *do* miss me.

Mrs. Muskat

Miss you? Not I. But the silly girls miss you. They're always asking for you. Well, are you going to be sensible and come back?

Liliom

And leave—her?

Mrs. Muskat

You beat her, don't you?

Liliom

No, I don't beat her. What's all this damn fool talk about beating her? I hit her once—that was all—and now the whole city seems to be talking about it. You don't call that beating her, do you?

Mrs. Muskat

All right, all right. I take it back. I don't want to get mixed up in it.

Liliom

Beating her! As if I'd beat her——

Mrs. Muskat

I can't make out why you're so concerned about her. You've been married to her two months—it's plain to see that you're sick of it—and out there is the carousel—and the show booths—and money—and you'd throw it all away. For what? Heavens, how can anyone be such a fool? [*Looks at him appraisingly.*] Where have you been all night? You look awful.

Liliom

It's no business of yours.

Mrs. Muskat

You never used to look like that. This life is telling on you. [*Pauses.*] Do you know—I've got a new organ.

LILIOM
[*Softly*.] I know.

MRS. MUSKAT
How did you know?

LILIOM
You can hear it—from here.

MRS. MUSKAT
It's a good one, eh?

LILIOM
[*Wistfully*.] Very good. Fine. It roars and snorts—so fine.

MRS. MUSKAT
You should hear it close by—it's heavenly. Even the carousel seems to know . . . it goes quicker. I got rid of those two horses—you know, the ones with the broken ears?

LILIOM
What have you put in their place?

MRS. MUSKAT
Guess.

LILIOM
Zebras?

MRS. MUSKAT
No—an automobile.

LILIOM

[*Transported.*]   An automobile———

MRS. MUSKAT

Yes. If you've got any sense you'll come back. What good are you doing here? Out there is your *art*, the only thing you're fit for. You are an artist, not a respectable married man.

LILIOM

Leave her—this little———

MRS. MUSKAT

She'll be better off. She'll go back and be a servant girl again. As for you—you're an artist and you belong among artists. All the beer you want, cigars, a krone a day and a gulden on Sunday, and the girls, Liliom, the girls—I've always treated you right, haven't I? I bought you a watch, and———

LILIOM

She's not that kind. She'd never be a servant girl again.

MRS. MUSKAT

I suppose you think she'd kill herself. Don't worry. Heavens, if every girl was to commit suicide just because her——— [*Finishes with a gesture.*]

Liliom

[*Stares at her a moment, considering, then with sudden, smiling animation.*] So the people don't like Hollinger?

Mrs. Muskat

You know very well they don't, you rascal.

Liliom

Well——

Mrs. Muskat

You've always been happy at the carousel. It's a great life—pretty girls and beer and cigars and music—a great life and an easy one. I'll tell you what—come back and I'll give you a ring that used to belong to my dear departed husband. Well, will you come?

Liliom

She's not that kind. She'd never be a servant girl again. But—but—for my part—if I decide—that needn't make any difference. I can go on living with her even if I do go back to my art——

Mrs. Muskat

My God!

Liliom

What's the matter?

Mrs. Muskat

Who ever heard of a married man—I suppose you think all girls would be pleased to know that you were running home to your wife every night. It's ridiculous! When the people found out they'd laugh themselves sick——

Liliom

I know what you want.

Mrs. Muskat

[*Refuses to meet his gaze.*] You flatter yourself.

Liliom

You'll give me that ring, too?

Mrs. Muskat

[*Pushes the hair back from his forehead.*] Yes.

Liliom

I'm not happy in this house.

Mrs. Muskat

[*Still stroking his hair.*] Nobody takes care of you. [*They are silent.* Julie *enters, carrying a cup of coffee.* Mrs. Muskat *removes her hand from* Liliom's *head. There is a pause.*]

Liliom

Do you want anything?

Julie

No. [*There is a pause. She exits slowly into the kitchen.*]

Mrs. Muskat

The old woman says there is a carpenter, a widower, who——

Liliom

I know—I know——

Julie

[*Reëntering.*] Liliom, before I forget, I have something to tell you.

Liliom

All right.

Julie

I've been wanting to tell you—in fact, I was going to tell you yesterday——

Liliom

Go ahead.

Julie

But I must tell you alone—if you'll come in—it will only take a minute.

Liliom

Don't you see I'm busy now? Here I am talking business and you interrupt with——

Julie

It'll only take a minute.

Liliom

Get out of here, or——

Julie

But I tell you it will only take a minute——

Liliom

Will you get out of here?

Julie

[*Courageously.*] No.

Liliom

[*Rising.*] What's that!

Julie

No.

Mrs. Muskat

[*Rises, too.*] Now don't start fighting. I'll go out and look at the photographs in the show-case a while and come back later for your answer. [*She exits at back.*]

JULIE

You can hit me again if you like—don't look at me like that. I'm not afraid of you. . . . I'm not afraid of anyone. I told you I had something to tell you.

LILIOM

Well, out with it—quick.

JULIE

I can't tell you so quick. Why don't you drink your coffee?

LILIOM

Is that what you wanted to tell me?

JULIE

No. By the time you've drunk your coffee I'll have told you.

LILIOM

[*Gets the coffee and sips it.*] Well?

JULIE

Yesterday my head ached—and you asked me——

LILIOM

Yes——

JULIE

Well—you see—that's what it is——

LILIOM

Are you sick?

JULIE

No. . . . But you wanted to know what my headaches came from—and you said I seemed—changed.

LILIOM

Did I? I guess I meant the carpenter.

JULIE

I've been—what? The carpenter? No. It's something entirely different—it's awful hard to tell—but you'll have to know sooner or later—I'm not a bit—scared—because it's a perfectly natural thing——

LILIOM

[*Puts the coffee cup on the table.*] What?

JULIE

When—when a man and woman—live together——

LILIOM

Yes.

JULIE

I'm going to have a baby. [*She exits swiftly at back. There is a pause.* FICSUR *appears at the open window and looks in.*]

Liliom

Ficsur! [*Ficsur sticks his head in.*] Say, Ficsur,—Julie is going to have a baby.

Ficsur

Yes? What of it?

Liliom

Nothing. [*Suddenly.*] Get out of here. [*Ficsur's head is quickly withdrawn. Mrs. Muskat reenters.*]

Mrs. Muskat

Has she gone?

Liliom

Yes.

Mrs. Muskat

I might as well give you ten kronen in advance. [*Opens her purse. Liliom takes up his coffee cup.*] Here you are. [*She proffers some coins. Liliom ignores her.*] Why don't you take it?

Liliom

[*Very nonchalantly, his cup poised ready to drink.*] Go home, Mrs. Muskat.

Mrs. Muskat

What's the matter with you?

LILIOM

Go home [*sips his coffee*] and let me finish my coffee in peace. Don't you see I'm at breakfast?

Mrs. Muskat

Have you gone crazy?

Liliom

Will you get out of here? [*Turns to her threateningly.*]

Mrs. Muskat

[*Restoring the coins to her purse.*] I'll never speak to you again as long as you live.

Liliom

That worries me a lot.

Mrs. Muskat

Good-bye!

Liliom

Good-bye. [*As she exits, he calls.*] Ficsur! [Ficsur *enters.*] Tell me, Ficsur. You said you knew a way to get a whole lot of money——

Ficsur

Sure I do.

Liliom

How much?

Ficsur

More than you ever had in your life before. You leave it to an old hand like me.

Mother Hollunder

[*Enters from the kitchen.*] In the morning he must have his coffee, and at noon his soup, and in the evening coffee again—and plenty of firewood—and I'm expected to furnish it all. Give me back my cup and saucer.

[*The show booths of the amusement-park have opened for business. The familiar noises begin to sound; clear above them all, but far in the distance, sounds the organ of the carousel.*]

Liliom

Now, Aunt Hollunder. [*From now until the fall of the curtain it is apparent that the sound of the organ makes him more and more uneasy.*]

Mother Hollunder

And you, you vagabond, get out of here this minute or I'll call my son——

Ficsur

I have nothing to do with the likes of him. He's too common. [*But he slinks out at back.*]

LILIOM
Aunt Hollunder!

MOTHER HOLLUNDER
What now?

LILIOM
When your son was born—when you brought him into the world——

MOTHER HOLLUNDER
Well?

LILIOM
Nothing.

MOTHER HOLLUNDER
[*Muttering as she exits.*] Sleep it off, you good-for-nothing lout. Drink and play cards all night long—that's all you know how to do—and take the bread out of poor people's mouths—you can do that, too. [*She exits.*]

LILIOM
Ficsur!

FICSUR
[*At the window.*] Julie's going to have a baby. You told me before.

LILIOM
This scheme—about the cashier of the leather factory—there's money in it——

FICSUR

Lots of money—but—it takes two to pull it off.

LILIOM

[*Meditatively.*] Yes. [*Uneasily.*] All right, Ficsur. Go away—and come back later.
[FICSUR *vanishes. The organ in the distant carousel drones incessantly.* LILIOM *listens a while, then goes to the door and calls.*]

LILIOM

Aunt Hollunder! [*With naïve joy.*] Julie's going to have a baby. [*Then he goes to the window, jumps on the sofa, looks out. Suddenly, in a voice that overtops the droning of the organ, he shouts as if addressing the far-off carousel.*] I'm going to be a father.

JULIE

[*Enters from the kitchen.*] Liliom! What's the matter? What's happened?

LILIOM

[*Coming down from the sofa.*] Nothing. [*Throws himself on the sofa, buries his face in the cushion.* JULIE *watches him a moment, comes over to him and covers him with a shawl. Then she goes on tip-toe to the door at back and remains standing in the doorway, looking out and listening to the droning of the organ.*]

THE CURTAIN FALLS

SCENE THREE

SCENE—*The setting is the same, later that afternoon.* LILIOM *is sitting opposite* FICSUR, *who is teaching him a song.* JULIE *hovers in the background, engaged in some household task.*

FICSUR

Listen now. Here's the third verse. [*Sings hoarsely.*]
"Look out, look out, my pretty lad,
 The damn police are on your trail;
 The nicest girl you ever had
 Has now commenced to weep and wail:
 Look out here comes the damn police,
 The damn police,
 The damn police,
 Look out here comes the damn police,
 They'll get you every time."

LILIOM

[*Sings.*]
"Look out, look out, my pretty lad,
 The damn police———"

Ficsur, Liliom

[*Sing together.*]
"Are on your trail
  The nicest girl you ever had
  Has now commenced to weep and wail."

Liliom

[*Alone.*]
"Look out here comes the damn police,
  The damn police,
  The damn police———"

[Julie, *troubled and uneasy, looks from one to the other, then exits into the kitchen.*]

Ficsur

[*When she has gone, comes quickly over to* Liliom *and speaks furtively.*] As you go down Franzen Street you come to the railroad embankment. Beyond that—all the way to the leather factory—there's not a thing in sight, not even a watchman's hut.

Liliom

And does he always come that way?

Ficsur

Yes. Not along the embankment, but down below along the path across the fields. Since last year he's been going alone. Before that he always used to have someone with him.

Liliom
Every Saturday?

Ficsur
Every Saturday.

Liliom
And the money? Where does he keep it?

Ficsur
In a leather bag. The whole week's pay for the workmen at the factory.

Liliom
Much?

Ficsur
Sixteen thousand kronen. Quite a haul, what?

Liliom
What's his name?

Ficsur
Linzman. He's a Jew.

Liliom
The cashier?

Ficsur

Yes—but when he gets a knife between his ribs—or if I smash his skull for him—he won't be a cashier any more.

Liliom

Does he have to be killed?

Ficsur

No, he doesn't *have* to be. He can give up the money *without* being killed—but most of these cashiers are peculiar—they'd rather be killed.

[Julie *reënters, pretends to get something on the other side of the room, then exits at back. During the ensuing dialogue she keeps coming in and out in the same way, showing plainly that she is suspicious and anxious. She attempts to overhear what they are saying and, in spite of their caution, does catch a word here and there, which adds to her disquiet.* Ficsur, *catching sight of her, abruptly changes the conversation.*]

Ficsur

And the next verse is:
"And when you're in the prison cell
They'll feed you bread and water."

Ficsur and Liliom

[*Sing together.*]
  "They'll make your little sweetheart tell
  Them all the things you brought her.
  Look out here comes the damn police,
  The damn police,
  The damn police.
  Look out here comes the damn police
  They'll get you every time."

Liliom

[*Sings alone.*]
  "And when you're in the prison cell
  They'll feed you bread and water——"
        [*Breaks off as* Julie *exits.*]
And when it's done, do we start right off for America?

Ficsur

No.

Liliom

What then?

Ficsur

We bury the money for six months. That's the usual time. And after the sixth month we dig it up again.

Liliom

And then?

FICSUR

Then you go on living just as usual for six months more—you don't touch a heller of the money.

LILIOM

In six months the baby will be born.

FICSUR

Then we'll take the baby with us, too. Three months before the time you'll go to work so as to be able to say you saved up your wages to get to America.

LILIOM

Which of us goes up and talks to him?

FICSUR

One of us talks to him with his mouth and the other talks with his knife. Depends on which you'd rather do. I'll tell you what—you talk to him with your mouth.

LILIOM

Do you hear that?

FICSUR

What?

LILIOM

Outside . . . like the rattle of swords. [FICSUR *listens. After a pause,* LILIOM *continues.*] What do I say to him?

Ficsur

You say good evening to him and: "Excuse me, sir; can you tell me the time?"

Liliom

And then what?

Ficsur

By that time I'll have stuck him—and then you take *your* knife—— [*He stops as a* Policeman *enters at back.*]

Policeman

Good-day!

Ficsur, Liliom

[*In unison.*] Good-day!

Ficsur

[*Calling toward the kitchen.*] Hey, photographer, come out. . . . Here's a customer. [*There is a pause. The* Policeman *waits.* Ficsur *sings softly.*]
"And when you're in the prison cell
They'll feed you bread and water
They'll make your little sweetheart tell."

Liliom, Ficsur

[*Sing together, low.*]
"Them all the things you brought her.
Look out here comes the——"

[*They hum the rest so as not to let the* POLICEMAN *hear the words "the damn police." As they sing,* MRS. HOLLUNDER *and her son enter.*]

POLICEMAN

Do you make cabinet photographs?

YOUNG HOLLUNDER

Certainly, sir. [*Points to a rack of photographs on the wall.*] Take your choice, sir. Would you like one full length?

POLICEMAN

Yes, full length. [MOTHER HOLLUNDER *pushes out the camera while her son poses the* POLICEMAN, *runs from him to the camera and back again, now altering the pose, now ducking under the black cloth and pushing the camera nearer. Meanwhile* MOTHER HOLLUNDER *has fetched a plate from the dark room and thrust it in the camera. While this is going on,* LILIOM *and* FICSUR. *their heads together, speak in very low tones.*]

LILIOM

Belong around here?

FICSUR

Not around here.

LILIOM

Where, then?

Ficsur

Suburban. [*There is a pause.*]

Liliom

[*Bursts out suddenly in a rather grotesquely childish and overstrained lament.*] O God, what a dirty life I'm leading—God, God!

Ficsur

[*Reassuring him benevolently.*] Over in America it will be better, all right.

Liliom

What's over there?

Ficsur

[*Virtuously.*] Factories . . . industries——

Young Hollunder

[*To the* Policeman.] Now, quite still, please. One, two, three. [*Deftly removes the cover of the lens and in a few seconds restores it.*] Thank you.

Mother Hollunder

The picture will be ready in five minutes.

Policeman

Good. I'll come back in five minutes. How much do I owe you?

Young Hollunder

[*With exaggerated deference.*] You don't need to pay in advance, Mr. Commissioner. [*The Policeman salutes condescendingly and exits at back. Mother Hollunder carries the plate into the dark room. Young Hollunder, after pushing the camera back in place, follows her.*]

Mother Hollunder

[*Muttering angrily as she passes Ficsur and Liliom.*] You hang around and dirty the whole place up! Why don't you go take a walk? Things are going so well with you that you have to sing, eh? [*Confronting Ficsur suddenly.*] Weren't you frightened sick when you saw the policeman?

Ficsur

[*With loathing.*] Go 'way, or I'll step on you. [*She exits into the dark room.*]

Liliom

They like Hollinger at the carousel?

Ficsur

I should say they do.

Liliom

Did you see the Muskat woman, too?

FICSUR

Sure. She takes care of Hollinger's hair.

LILIOM

Combs his hair?

FICSUR

She fixes him all up.

LILIOM

Let her fix him all she likes.

FICSUR

[*Urging him toward the kitchen door.*] Go on. Now's your chance.

LILIOM

What for?

FICSUR

To get the knife.

LILIOM

What knife?

FICSUR

The kitchen knife. I've got a pocket-knife, but if he shows fight, we'll let him have the big knife.

LILIOM

What for? If he gets ugly, I'll bat him one over the head that'll make him squint for the rest of his life.

Ficsur

You've got to have something on you. You can't slit his throat with a bat over the head.

Liliom

Must his throat be slit?

Ficsur

No, it *mustn't*. But if he asks for it. [*There is a pause.*] You'd like to sail on the big steamer, wouldn't you? And you want to see the factories over there, don't you? But you're not willing to inconvenience yourself a little for them.

Liliom

If I take the knife, Julie will see me.

Ficsur

Take it so she won't see you.

Liliom

[*Advances a few paces toward the kitchen. The* Policeman *enters at back.* Liliom *knocks on the door of the dark room.*] Here's the policeman!

Mother Hollunder

[*Coming out.*] One minute more, please. Just a minute. [*She reënters the dark room.* Liliom *hesitates a moment, then exits into the kitchen. The* POLICEMAN *scrutinizes* FICSUR *mockingly.* FICSUR *returns his stare, walks a few paces toward him, then deliberately turns his back. Suddenly he wheels around, points at the* POLICEMAN *and addresses him in a teasing, childish tone.*] Christiana Street at the corner of Retti!

POLICEMAN

[*Amazed, self-conscious.*] How do you know that?

FICSUR

I used to practice my profession in that neighborhood.

POLICEMAN

What is your profession?

FICSUR

Professor of pianola—— [*The* POLICEMAN *glares, aware that the man is joking with him, twirls his moustache indignantly.* YOUNG HOLLUNDER *comes out of the dark room and gives him the finished pictures.*]

YOUNG HOLLUNDER

Here you are, sir. [*The* POLICEMAN *examines the photographs, pays for them, starts to go, stops, glares at* FICSUR *and exits. When he is gone,* FIC-

sur *goes to the doorway and looks out after him.*
Young Hollunder *exits.* Liliom *reënters, buttoning his coat.*]

Ficsur

[*Turns, sees* Liliom.] What are you staring at?

Liliom

I'm not staring.

Ficsur

What then are you doing?

Liliom

I'm thinking it over.

Ficsur

[*Comes very close to him.*] Tell me then—what will you say to him?

Liliom

[*Unsteadily.*] I'll say—"Good evening—Excuse me, sir—Can you tell me the time?" And suppose he answers me, what do I say to him?

Ficsur

He won't answer you.

Liliom

Don't you think so?

Ficsur

No. [*Feeling for the knife under* Liliom's *coat.*] Where is it? Where did you put it?

Liliom

[*Stonily.*] Left side.

Ficsur

That's right—over your heart. [*Feels it.*] Ah—there it is—there—there's the blade—quite a big fellow, isn't it—ah, here it begins to get narrower. [*Reaches the tip of the knife.*] And here is its eye—that's what it sees with. [Julie *enters from the kitchen, passes them slowly, watching them in silent terror, then stops.* Ficsur *nudges* Liliom.] Sing, come on, sing!

Liliom

[*In a quavering voice.*]
   "Look out for the damn police."

Ficsur

[*Joining in, cheerily, loudly, marking time with the swaying of his body.*]
   "Look out, look out, my pretty lad."

Liliom

"—look out, my pretty lad." [Julie *goes out at back.* Liliom's *glance follows her. When she has gone, he turns to* Ficsur.] At night—in my dreams—if his ghost comes back—what will I do then?

Ficsur

His ghost won't never come back.

Liliom

Why not?

Ficsur

A Jew's ghost don't come back.

Liliom

Well then—afterwards——

Ficsur

[*Impatiently.*] What do you mean—afterwards?

Liliom

In the next world—when I come up before the Lord God—what'll I say then?

Ficsur

The likes of you will never come up before Him.

Liliom

Why not?

Ficsur

Have you ever come up before the high court?

Liliom
No.

Ficsur
Our kind comes up before the police magistrate—and the highest we *ever* get is the criminal court.

Liliom
Will it be the same in the next world?

Ficsur
Just the same. We'll come up before a police magistrate, same as we did in this world.

Liliom
A police magistrate?

Ficsur
Sure. For the rich folks—the Heavenly Court. For us poor people—only a police magistrate. For the rich folks—fine music and angels. For us——

Liliom
For us?

Ficsur
For us, my son, there's only justice. In the next world there'll be lots of justice, yes, nothing but justice. And where there's justice there must be police magistrates; and where there're police magistrates, people like us get——

LILIOM

[*Interrupting.*] Good evening. Excuse me, sir, can you tell me the time? [*Lays his hand over his heart.*]

FICSUR

What do you put your hand there for?

LILIOM

My heart is jumping—under the knife.

FICSUR

Put it on the other side then. [*Looks out at the sky.*] It's time we started—we'll walk slow——

LILIOM

It's too early.

FICSUR

Come on. [*As they are about to go,* JULIE *appears in the doorway at back, obstructing the way.*]

JULIE

Where are you going with him?

LILIOM

Where am I going with him?

JULIE

Stay home.

LILIOM

No.

JULIE

Stay home. It's going to rain soon, and you'll get wet.

FICSUR

It won't rain.

JULIE

How do you know?

FICSUR

I always get notice in advance.

JULIE

Stay home. This evening the carpenter's coming. I've asked him to give you work.

LILIOM

I'm not a carpenter.

JULIE

[*More and more anxious, though she tries to conceal it.*] Stay home. Marie's coming with her intended to have their picture taken. She wants to introduce us to her intended husband.

LILIOM

I've seen enough intended husbands——

JULIE

Stay home. Marie's bringing some money, and I'll give it all to you.

LILIOM

[*Approaching the door.*] I'm going—for a walk—with Ficsur. We'll be right back.

JULIE

[*Forcing a smile to keep back her tears.*] If you stay home, I'll get you a glass of beer—or wine, if you prefer.

FICSUR

Coming or not?

JULIE

I'm not angry with you any more for hitting me.

LILIOM

[*Gruffly, but his gruffness is simulated to hide the fact that he cannot bear the sight of her suffering.*] Stand out of the way—or I'll—— [*He clenches his fist.*] Let me out!

JULIE

[*Trembling.*] What have you got under your coat?

LILIOM

[*Produces from his pocket a greasy pack of cards.*] Cards.

JULIE

[*Trembling, speaks very low.*] What's under your coat?

LILIOM

Let me out!

JULIE

[*Obstructing the way. Speaks quickly, eagerly, in a last effort to detain him.*] Marie's intended knows about a place for a married couple without children to be caretakers of a house on Arader Street. Rent free, a kitchen of your own, and the privilege of keeping chickens——

LILIOM

Get out of the way! [JULIE *stands aside.* LILIOM *exits.* FICSUR *follows him.* JULIE *remains standing meditatively in the doorway.* MOTHER HOLLUNDER *comes out of the kitchen.*]

MOTHER HOLLUNDER

I can't find my kitchen knife anywhere. Have you seen anything of it?

JULIE

[*Horrified.*] No.

MOTHER HOLLUNDER

It was on the kitchen table just a few minutes ago. No one was in there except Liliom.

JULIE

He didn't take it.

MOTHER HOLLUNDER

No one else was in there.

JULIE

What would Liliom want with a kitchen knife?

MOTHER HOLLUNDER

He'd sell it and spend the money on drink.

JULIE

It just so happens—see how unjust you are to him—it just so happens that I went through all of Liliom's pockets just now—I wanted to see if he had any money on him. But he had nothing but a pack of cards.

MOTHER HOLLUNDER

[*Returns to the kitchen, grumbling.*] Cards in his pocket—cards! The fine gentlemen have evidently gone off to their club to play a little game. [*She exits. After a pause* MARIE, *happy and beaming, appears in the doorway at back, and enters, followed by* WOLF.]

Marie

Here we are! [*She takes* Wolf *by the hand and leads him, grinning shyly, to* Julie, *who has turned at her call.*] Hello!

Julie

Hello.

Marie

Well, we're here.

Julie

Yes.

Wolf

[*Bows awkwardly and extends his hand.*] My name is Wolf Beifeld.

Julie

My name is Julie Zeller. [*They shake hands. There is an embarrassed silence. Then, to relieve the situation,* Wolf *takes* Julie's *hand again and shakes it vigorously.*]

Marie

Well—this is Wolf.

Wolf

Yes.

Julie

Yes. [*Another awkward silence.*]

Marie

Where is Liliom?

WOLF

Yes, where is your husband?

JULIE

He's out.

MARIE

Where?

JULIE

Just for a walk.

MARIE

Is he?

JULIE

Yes.

WOLF

Oh! [*Another silence.*]

MARIE

Wolf's got a new place. After the first of the month he won't have to stand outside any more. He's going to work in a club after the first of the month.

WOLF

[*Apologetically.*] She don't know yet how to explain these things just right—hehehe—— Beginning the first I'm to be second steward at the Burger Club—a good job, if one conducts oneself properly.

JULIE

Yes?

WOLF

The pay—is quite good—but the main thing is the tips. When they play cards there's always a bit for the steward. The tips, I may say, amount to twenty, even thirty kronen every night.

MARIE

Yes.

WOLF

We've rented two rooms for ourselves to start with—and if things go well——

MARIE

Then we'll buy a house in the country.

WOLF

If one only tends to business and keeps honest. Of course, in the country we'll miss the city life, but if the good Lord sends us children—it's much healthier for children in the country. [*There is a brief pause.*]

MARIE

Wolf's nice looking, isn't he?

JULIE

Yes.

MARIE

And he's a good boy, Wolf.

JULIE
Yes.

MARIE
The only thing is—he's a Jew.

JULIE
Oh, well, you can get used to that.

MARIE
Well, aren't you going to wish us luck?

JULIE
Of course I do. [*She embraces* MARIE.]

MARIE
And aren't you going to kiss Wolf, too?

JULIE
Him, too. [*She embraces* WOLF, *remains quite still a moment, her head resting on his shoulder.*]

WOLF
Why are you crying, my dear Mrs.—— [*He looks questioningly at* MARIE *over* JULIE's *shoulder.*]

MARIE
Because she has such a good heart. [*She becomes sentimental, too.*]

WOLF

[*Touched.*] We thank you for your heartfelt sympathy—— [*He cannot restrain his own tears. There is a pause before* MOTHER HOLLUNDER *and her son enter.* YOUNG HOLLUNDER *immediately busies himself with the camera.*]

MOTHER HOLLUNDER

Now if you don't mind, we'll do it right away, before it gets too dark. [*She leads* MARIE *and* WOLF *into position before the background-screen. Here they immediately fall into an awkward pose, smiling mechanically.*] Full length?

MARIE

Please. Both figures full length.

MOTHER HOLLUNDER

Bride and groom?

MARIE

Yes.

MOTHER HOLLUNDER, YOUNG HOLLUNDER

[*Speak in unison, in loud professionally-expressionless tones.*] The lady looks at the gentleman and the gentleman looks straight into the camera.

Mother Hollunder

[*Poses first* Marie, *then* Wolf.] Now, if you please.

Young Hollunder

[*Who has crept under the black cloth, calls in muffled tones.*] That's good—that's very good!

Marie

[*Stonily rigid, but very happy, trying to speak without altering her expression.*] Julie, dear, do we look all right?

Julie

Yes, dear.

Young Hollunder

Now, if you please, hold still. I'll count up to three, and then you must hold perfectly still. [*Grasps the cover of the lens and calls threateningly.*] One—two—three! [*He removes the cover; there is utter silence. But as he speaks the word "one" there is heard, very faintly in the distance, the refrain of the thieves' song which* Ficsur *and* Liliom *have been singing. The refrain continues until the fall of the curtain. As he speaks the word "three" everybody is perfectly rigid save* Julie, *who lets her head sink slowly to the table. The distant refrain dies out.*]

The Curtain Falls

SCENE FOUR

SCENE—*In the fields on the outskirts of the city. At back a railroad embankment crosses the stage obliquely. At Center of the embankment stands a red and white signal flag, and near it a little red signal lamp which is not yet lighted. Here also a wooden stairway leads up to the embankment.*

At the foot of the embankment to the right is a pile of used railroad ties. In the background a telegraph pole, beyond it a view of trees, fences and fields; still further back a factory building and a cluster of little dwellings.

It is six o'clock of the same afternoon. Dusk has begun to fall.

LILIOM *and* FICSUR *are discovered on the stairway looking after the train which has just passed.*

LILIOM

Can you still hear it snort?

FICSUR

Listen! [*They watch the vanishing train.*]

LILIOM

If you put your ear on the tracks you can hear it go all the way to Vienna.

FICSUR

Huh!

LILIOM

The one that just puffed past us—it goes all the way to Vienna.

FICSUR

No further?

LILIOM

Yes—further, too. [*There is a pause.*]

FICSUR

It must be near six. [*As* LILIOM *ascends the steps.*] Where are you going?

LILIOM

Don't be afraid. I'm not giving you the slip.

FICSUR

Why should you give me the slip? That cashier has sixteen thousand kronen on him. Just be patient till he comes, then you can talk to him, nice and polite.

LILIOM

I say, "Good evening—excuse me, sir; what time is it?"

FICSUR

Then he tells you what time it is.

LILIOM

Suppose he don't come?

FICSUR

[*Coming down the steps.*] Nonsense! He's got to come. He pays off the workmen every Saturday. And this is Saturday, ain't it? [LILIOM *has ascended to the top of the stairway and is gazing along the tracks.*] What are you looking at up there?

LILIOM

The tracks go on and on—there's no end to them.

FICSUR

What's that to stare about?

LILIOM

Nothing—only I always look after the train. When you stand down there at night it snorts past you, and spits down.

FICSUR

Spits?

LILIOM

Yes, the engine. It spits down. And then the whole train rattles past and away—and you stand there—spat on—but it draws your eyes along with it.

FICSUR

Draws your eyes along?

LILIOM

Yes—whether you want to or not, you've got to look after it—as long as the tiniest bit of it is in sight.

FICSUR

Swell people sit in it.

LILIOM

And read newspapers.

FICSUR

And smoke cigars.

LILIOM

And inhale the smoke. [*There is a short silence.*]

FICSUR

Is he coming?

LILIOM

Not yet. [*Silence again.* LILIOM *comes down, speaks low, confidentially.*] Do you hear the telegraph wires?

FICSUR

I hear them when the wind blows.

Liliom

Even when the wind doesn't blow you can hear them humming, humming—— People talk through them.

Ficsur

Who?

Liliom

Jews.

Ficsur

No—they telegraph.

Liliom

They talk through them and from some other place they get answered. And it all goes through the iron strings—that's why they hum like that—they hum-m——

Ficsur

What do they hum?

Liliom

They hum! ninety-nine, ninety-nine. Just listen.

Ficsur

What for?

Liliom

That sparrow's listening, too. He's cocked one eye and looks at me as if to say: "I'd like to know what they're talking about."

FICSUR

You're looking at a bird?

LILIOM

He's looking at me, too.

FICSUR

Listen, you're sick! There's something the matter with you. Do you know what it is? Money. That bird has no money, either; that's why he cocks his eye.

LILIOM

Maybe.

FICSUR

Whoever has money don't cock his eye.

LILIOM

What then does he do?

FICSUR

He does most anything he wants. But nobody works unless he has money. We'll soon have money ourselves.

LILIOM

I say, "Good evening. Excuse me, sir, can you tell me what time it is!"

FICSUR

He's not coming yet. Got the cards? [LILIOM *gives him the pack of cards.*] Got any money?

LILIOM

[*Takes some coins from his trousers pocket and counts.*] Eleven.

FICSUR

[*Sits astride on the pile of ties and looks off left.*] All right—eleven.

LILIOM

[*Sitting astride on the ties facing him.*] Put it up.

FICSUR

[*Puts the money on the ties; rapidly shuffles the cards.*] We'll play twenty-one. I'll bank. [*He deals deftly.*]

LILIOM

[*Looks at his card.*] Good. I'll bet the bank.

FICSUR

Must have an ace! [*Deals him a second card.*]

LILIOM

Another one. [*He gets another card.*] Another. [*Gets still another.*] Over! [*Throws down his cards.* FICSUR *gathers in the money.*] Come on!

FICSUR

Come on what? Got no more money, have you?

LILIOM

No.

FICSUR

Then the game's over—unless you want to——

LILIOM

What?

FICSUR

Play on credit.

LILIOM

You'll trust me?

FICSUR

No—but—I'll deduct it.

LILIOM

Deduct it from what?

FICSUR

From your share of the money. If *you* win you deduct from my share.

LILIOM

[*Looks over his shoulder to see if the cashier is coming; nervous and ashamed.*] All right. How much is bank?

LILIOM 117

Ficsur

That cashier is bringing us sixteen thousand kronen. Eight thousand of that is mine. Well, then, the bank is eight thousand.

Liliom

Good.

Ficsur

Whoever has the most luck will have the most money. [*He deals.*]

Liliom

Six hundred kronen. [Ficsur *gives him another card.*] Enough.

Ficsur

[*Laying out his own cards.*] Twenty-one. [*He shuffles rapidly.*]

Liliom

[*Moves excitedly nearer to* Ficsur.] Well, then, double or nothing.

Ficsur

[*Dealing.*] Double or nothing.

Liliom

[*Gets a card.*] Enough.

Ficsur

[*Laying out his own cards.*] Twenty-one. [*Shuffles rapidly again.*]

LILIOM

[*In alarm.*] You're not—cheating?

FICSUR

Me? Do I look like a cheat? [*Deals the cards again.*]

LILIOM

[*Glances nervously over his shoulder.*] A thousand.

FICSUR

[*Nonchalantly.*] Kronen?

LILIOM

Kronen. [*He gets a card.*] Another one. [*Gets another card.*] Over again! [*Like an inexperienced gambler who is losing heavily,* LILIOM *is very nervous. He plays dazedly, wildly, irrationally. From now on it is apparent that his only thought is to win his money back.*]

FICSUR

That makes twelve hundred you owe.

LILIOM

Double or nothing. [*He gets a card. He is greatly excited.*] Another one. [*Gets another card.*] Another. [*Throws down three cards.*]

Ficsur

[*Bends over and adds up the sum on the ground.*] Ten—fourteen—twenty-three—— You owe two thousand, four hundred.

Liliom

Now what?

Ficsur

[*Takes a card out of the deck and gives it to him.*] Here's the red ace. You can play double or nothing again.

Liliom

[*Eagerly.*] Good. [*Gets another card.*] Enough.

Ficsur

[*Turns up his own cards.*] Nineteen.

Liliom

You win again. [*Almost imploring.*] Give me an ace again. Give me the green one. [*Takes a card.*] Double or nothing.

Ficsur

Not any more.

Liliom

Why not?

Ficsur

Because if you lose you won't be able to pay. Double would be nine thousand six hundred. And you've only got eight thousand altogether.

Liliom

[*Greatly excited.*] That—that—I call that—a dirty trick!

Ficsur

Three thousand, two hundred. That's all you can put up.

Liliom

[*Eagerly.*] All right, then—three thousand, two hundred. [Ficsur *deals him a card.*] Enough.

Ficsur

I've got an ace myself. Now we'll have to take our time and squeeze 'em. [Liliom *pushes closer to him as he takes up his cards and slowly, intently unfolds them.*] Twenty-one. [*He quickly puts the cards in his pocket. There is a pause.*]

Liliom

Now—now—I'll tell you now—you're a crook, a low-down——[*Now* Linzman *enters at Right. He is a strong, robust, red-bearded Jew about 40 years of age. At his side he carries a leather bag slung by a strap from his shoulder.* Ficsur *coughs warn-*

ingly, moves to the right between LINZMAN *and the embankment, pauses just behind* LINZMAN *and follows him.* LILIOM *stands bewildered a few paces to the left of the railroad ties. He finds himself facing* LINZMAN. *Trembling in every limb.*] Good evening. Excuse me, sir, can you tell me the time? [FICSUR *springs silently at* LINZMAN, *the little knife in his right hand. But* LINZMAN *catches* FICSUR'S *right hand with his own left and forces* FICSUR *to his knees. Simultaneously* LINZMAN *thrusts his right hand into his coat pocket and produces a revolver which he points at* LILIOM'S *breast.* LILIOM *is standing two paces away from the revolver. There is a long pause.*]

LINZMAN

[*In a low, even voice.*] It is twenty-five minutes past six. [*Pauses, looks ironically down at* FICSUR.] It's lucky I grabbed the hand with the knife instead of the other one. [*Pauses again, looks appraisingly from one to the other.*] Two fine birds! [*To* FICSUR.] I should live so—Rothschild has more luck than you. [*To* LILIOM.] I'd advise you to keep nice and quiet. If you make one move, you'll get two bullets in you. Just look into the barrel. You'll see some little things in there made of lead.

FICSUR

Let me go. I didn't do anything.

Linzman

[*Mockingly shakes the hand which still holds the knife.*] And this? What do you call this? Oh, yes, I know. You thought I had an apple in my pocket, and you wanted to peel it. That's it. Forgive me for my error. I beg your pardon, sir.

Liliom

But I—I——

Linzman

Yes, my son, I know. It's so simple. You only asked what time it is. Well, it's twenty-five minutes after six.

Ficsur

Let us go, honorable sir. We didn't do anything to you.

Linzman

In the first place, my son, I'm not an honorable sir. In the second place, for the same money, you could have said Your Excellency. But in the third place you'll find it very hard to beg off by flattering me.

Liliom

But I—*I* really didn't do anything to you.

Linzman

Look behind you, my boy. Don't be afraid. Look behind you, but don't run away or I'll have to shoot you down. [LILIOM *turns his head slowly around.*] Who's coming up there?

LILIOM

[*Looking at* LINZMAN.] Policemen.

LINZMAN

[*To* FICSUR.] You hold still, or—— [*To* LILIOM *teasingly.*] How many policemen are there?

LILIOM

[*His eyes cast down.*] Two.

LINZMAN

And what are the policemen sitting on?

LILIOM

Horses.

LINZMAN

And which can run faster, a horse or a man?

LILIOM

A horse.

LINZMAN

There, you see. It would be hard to get away now. [*Laughs.*] I never saw such an unlucky pair of highway robbers. I can't imagine worse luck. Just today I had to put a pistol in my pocket. And even if I hadn't—old Linzman is a match for four like you. But even that isn't all. Did you happen to notice, you oxen, what direction I came from? From the factory, didn't I? When I *went* there I had a nice bit of money with me. Sixteen thousand crowns! But now—not a heller. [*Calls off left.*] Hey, come quicker, will you? This fellow is pulling pretty strong. [Ficsur *frees himself with a mighty wrench and darts rapidly off. As* Linzman *aims his pistol at the vanishing* Ficsur, Liliom *runs up the steps to the embankment.* Linzman *hesitates, perceives that* Liliom *is the better target, points the pistol at him.*] Stop, or I'll shoot! [*Calls off left to the* Policemen.] Why don't you come down off your horses? [*His pistol is leveled at* Liliom, *who stands on the embankment, facing the audience. From the left on the embankment a* Policeman *appears, revolver in hand.*]

First Policeman

Stop!

Linzman

Well, my boy, do you still want to know what time it is? From ten to twelve years in prison!

Liliom

You won't get me! [Linzman *laughs derisively.* Liliom *is now three or four paces from the* Policeman *and equally distant from* Linzman. *His face is uplifted to the sky. He bursts into laughter, half defiant, half self-pitying, and takes the kitchen knife from under his coat.*] Julie—— [*The ring of farewell is in the word. He turns sideways, thrusts the knife deep in his breast, sways, falls and rolls down the far side of the embankment. There is a long pause. From the left up on the embankment come the* TWO POLICEMEN.]

LINZMAN

What's the matter? [*The* FIRST POLICEMAN *comes along the embankment as far as the steps, looks down in the opposite side, then climbs down at about the spot where* LILIOM *disappeared.* LINZMAN *and the other* POLICEMAN *mount the embankment and look down on him.*] Stabbed himself?

VOICE OF FIRST POLICEMAN

Yes—and he seems to have made a thorough job of it.

LINZMAN

[*Excitedly to the* SECOND POLICEMAN.] I'll go and telephone to the hospital. [*He runs down the steps and exits at left.*]

SECOND POLICEMAN

Go to Eisler's grocery store and telephone to the factory from there. They've a doctor there, too.

[*Calling down to the other* POLICEMAN.] I'm going to tie up the horses. [*Comes down the steps and exits at left. The stage is empty. There is a pause. The little red signal lamp is lit.*]

VOICE OF FIRST POLICEMAN

Hey, Stephan!

VOICE OF SECOND POLICEMAN

What?

VOICE OF FIRST POLICEMAN

Shall I pull the knife out of his chest?

VOICE OF SECOND POLICEMAN

Better not, or he may bleed to death. [*There is a pause.*]

VOICE OF FIRST POLICEMAN

Stephan!

VOICE OF SECOND POLICEMAN

Yes.

VOICE OF FIRST POLICEMAN

Lot of mosquitoes around here.

VOICE OF SECOND POLICEMAN

Yes.

VOICE OF FIRST POLICEMAN

Got a cigar?

Voice of Second Policeman

No. [*There is a pause. The* First Policeman *appears over the opposite side of the embankment.*]

First Policeman

A lot of good the new pay-schedule's done us—made things worse than they used to be—we *get* more but we *have* less than we ever had. If the Government could be made to realize that. It's a thankless job at best. You work hard year after year, you get gray in the service, and slowly you die—yes.

Second Policeman

That's right.

First Policeman

Yes. [*In the distance is heard the bell of the signal tower.*]

The Curtain Falls

SCENE FIVE

SCENE—*The photographic "studio" a half hour later that same evening.*

MOTHER HOLLUNDER, her son, MARIE and WOLF stand in a group back right, their heads together. JULIE stands apart from them, a few paces to the left.

YOUNG HOLLUNDER

[*Who has just come in, tells his story excitedly.*] They're bringing him now. Two workmen from the factory are carrying him on a stretcher.

WOLF

Where is the doctor?

YOUNG HOLLUNDER

A policeman telephoned to headquarters. The police-surgeon ought to be here any minute.

MARIE

Maybe they'll pull him through after all.

LILIOM

YOUNG HOLLUNDER
He stabbed himself too deep in his chest. But he's still breathing. He can still talk, too, but very faintly. At first he lay there unconscious, but when they put him on the stretcher he came to.

WOLF
That was from the shaking.

MARIE
We'd better make room. [*They make room. Two workmen carry in* LILIOM *on a stretcher which has four legs and stands about as high as a bed. They put the stretcher at left directly in front of the sofa, so that the head is at right and the foot at left. Then they unobtrusively join the group at the door. Later, they go out.* JULIE *is standing at the side of the stretcher, where, without moving, she can see* LILIOM'S *face. The others crowd emotionally together near the door. The* FIRST POLICEMAN *enters.*]

FIRST POLICEMAN
Are you his wife?

JULIE
Yes.

FIRST POLICEMAN
The doctor at the factory who bandaged him up forbade us to take him to the hospital.—Dangerous

to move him that far. What he needs now is rest. Just let him be until the police-surgeon comes. [*To the group near the door.*] He's not to be disturbed. [*They make way for him. He exits. There is a pause.*]

Wolf

[*Gently urging the others out.*] Please—it's best if we all get out of here now. We'll only be in the way.

Marie

[*To Julie.*] Julie, what do you think? [Julie *looks at her without answering.*] Julie, can I do anything to help? [Julie *does not answer.*] We'll be just outside on the bench if you want us. [Mother Hollunder *and her son have gone out when first requested. Now* Marie *and* Wolf *exit, too.* Julie *sits on the edge of the stretcher and looks at* Liliom. *He stretches his hand out to her. She clasps it. It is not quite dark yet. Both of them can still be plainly seen.*]

Liliom

[*Raises himself with difficulty; speaks lightly at first, but later soberly, defiantly.*] Little—Julie—there's something—I want to tell you—like when you go to a restaurant—and you've finished eating—and it's time—to pay—then you have to count up everything—everything you owe—well—I beat you—not because I was mad at you—no—only because I can't bear to see anyone crying. You always cried—on my account—and, well, you see,—I never learned a trade—what kind of a caretaker would I make? But anyhow—I wasn't going back to the carousel to fool with the girls. No, I spit on them all—understand?

Julie

Yes.

Liliom

And—as for Hollinger—he's good enough—Mrs. Muskat can get along all right with him. The jokes he tells are mine—and the people laugh when he tells them—but I don't care.—I didn't give you anything—no home—not even the food you ate—but you don't understand.—It's true I'm not much good—but I couldn't be a caretaker—and so I thought maybe it would be better over there—in America—do you see?

Julie

Yes.

Liliom

I'm not asking—forgiveness—I don't do that—I don't. Tell the baby—if you like.

Julie

Yes.

Liliom

Tell the baby—I wasn't much good—but tell him —if you ever talk about me—tell him—I thought —perhaps—over in America—but that's no affair of yours. I'm not asking forgiveness. For my part the police can come now.—If it's a boy—if it's a girl. —Perhaps I'll see the Lord God today.—Do you think I'll see Him?

Julie

Yes.

Liliom

I'm not afraid—of the police Up There—if they'll only let me come up in front of the Lord God Himself—not like down here where an officer stops you at the door. If the carpenter asks you—yes—be his wife—marry him. And the child—tell him he's his father.—He'll believe you—won't he?

Julie

Yes.

Liliom

When I beat you—I was right.—You mustn't always think—you mustn't always be right.—Liliom can be right once, too.—It's all the same to me who was right.—It's so dumb. Nobody's right—but they all think they are right.—A lot they know!

Julie

Yes.

Liliom

Julie—come—hold my hand tight.

Julie

I'm holding it tight—all the time.

Liliom

Tighter, still tighter—I'm going—— [*Pauses.*] Julie——

Julie

Good-bye. [Liliom *sinks slowly back and dies.* Julie *frees her hand.* The Doctor *enters with the* First Policeman.]

Doctor

Good evening. His wife?

Julie

Yes, sir. [*Behind the* Doctor *and* Policeman *enter* Marie, Wolf, Mother Hollunder, Young Hollunder *and* Mrs. Muskat. *They remain respectfully at the doorway. The* Doctor *bends over* Liliom *and examines him.*]

Doctor

A light, if you please. [Julie *fetches a burning candle from the dark room. The* Doctor *examines* Liliom *briefly in the candle-light, then turns suddenly away.*] Have you pen and ink?

WOLF

[*Proffering a pen.*] A fountain-pen—American——

DOCTOR

[*Takes a printed form from his pocket; speaks as he writes out the death-certificate at the little table.*] My poor woman, your husband is dead—there's nothing to be done for him—the good God will help him now—I'll leave this certificate with you. You will give it to the people from the hospital when they come—I'll arrange for the body to be removed at once. [*Rises.*] Please give me a towel and soap.

POLICEMAN

I've got them for you out here, sir. [*Points to door at back.*]

DOCTOR

God be with you, my good woman.

JULIE

Thank you, sir. [*The* DOCTOR *and* POLICEMAN *exit. The others slowly draw nearer.*]

MARIE

Poor Julie. May he rest in peace, poor man, but as for you—please don't be angry with me for saying it—but you're better off this way.

Mother Hollunder

He is better off, the poor fellow, and so are you.

Marie

Much better, Julie . . . you are young . . . and one of these days some good man will come along. Am I right?

Wolf

She's right.

Marie

Julie, tell me, am I right?

Julie

You are right, dear; you are very good.

Young Hollunder

There's a good man—the carpenter. Oh, I can speak of it now. He comes here every day on some excuse or other—and he never fails to ask for you.

Marie

A widower—with two children.

Mother Hollunder

He's better off, poor fellow—and so are you. He was a bad man.

Marie

He wasn't good-hearted. Was he, Wolf?

Wolf

No, I must say, he really wasn't. No, Liliom wasn't a good man. A good man doesn't strike a woman.

Marie

Am I right? Tell me, Julie, am I right?

Julie

You are right, dear.

Young Hollunder

It's really a good thing for her it happened.

Mother Hollunder

He's better off—and so is she.

Wolf

Now you have your freedom again. How old are you?

Julie

Eighteen.

Wolf

Eighteen. A mere child! Am I right?

Julie

You are right, Wolf. You are kind.

Young Hollunder

Lucky for you it happened, isn't it?

JULIE

Yes.

YOUNG HOLLUNDER

All you had before was bad luck. If it weren't for my mother you wouldn't have had a roof over your head or a bite to eat—and now Autumn's coming and Winter. You couldn't have lived in this shack in the Winter time, could you?

MARIE

Certainly not! You'd have frozen like the birds in the fields. Am I right, Julie?

JULIE

Yes, Marie.

MARIE

A year from now you will have forgotten all about him, won't you?

JULIE

You are right, Marie.

WOLF

If you need anything, count on us. We'll go now. But tomorrow morning we'll be back. Come, Marie. God be with you. [*Offers* JULIE *his hand.*]

JULIE

God be with you.

MARIE

[*Embraces* JULIE, *weeping.*] It's the best thing that could have happened to you, Julie, the best thing.

JULIE

Don't cry, Marie. [MARIE *and* WOLF *exit.*]

MOTHER HOLLUNDER

I'll make a little black coffee. You haven't had a thing to eat today. Then you'll come home with us. [MOTHER HOLLUNDER *and her son exit.* MRS. MUSKAT *comes over to* JULIE.]

MRS. MUSKAT

Would you mind if I—looked at him?

JULIE

He used to work for you.

MRS. MUSKAT

[*Contemplates the body; turns to* JULIE.] Won't you make up with me?

JULIE

I wasn't angry with you.

MRS. MUSKAT

But you were. Let's make it up.

Julie

[*Raising her voice eagerly, almost triumphantly.*] I've nothing to make up with *you*.

Mrs. Muskat

But I have with you. Everyone says hard things against the poor dead boy—except us two. You don't say he was bad.

Julie

[*Raising her voice yet higher, this time on a defiant, wholly triumphant note.*] Yes, I do.

Mrs. Muskat

I understand, my child. But he beat me, too. What does that matter? I've forgotten it.

Julie

[*From now on answers her coldly, drily, without looking at her.*] That's your own affair.

Mrs. Muskat

If I can help you in any way——

Julie

There's nothing I need.

Mrs. Muskat

I still owe him two kronen, back pay.

JULIE

You should have paid him.

MRS. MUSKAT

Now that the poor fellow is dead I thought perhaps it would be the same if I paid you.

JULIE

I've nothing to do with it.

MRS. MUSKAT

All right. Please don't think I'm trying to force myself on you. I stayed because we two are the only ones on earth who loved him. That's why I thought we ought to stick together.

JULIE

No, thank you.

MRS. MUSKAT

Then you couldn't have loved him as I did.

JULIE

No.

MRS. MUSKAT

I loved him better.

JULIE

Yes.

MRS. MUSKAT

Good-bye.

JULIE

Good-bye. [MRS. MUSKAT *exits.* JULIE *puts the candle on the table near* LILIOM'S *head, sits on the edge of the stretcher, looks into the dead man's face and caresses it tenderly.*] Sleep, Liliom, sleep—it's no business of hers—I never even told you—but now I'll tell you—now I'll tell you—you bad, quick-tempered, rough, unhappy, wicked—*dear* boy—sleep peacefully, Liliom—they can't understand how I feel—I can't even explain to you—not even to you—how I feel—you'd only laugh at me—but you can't hear me any more. [*Between tender motherliness and reproach, yet with great love in her voice.*] It was wicked of you to beat me—on the breast and on the head and face—but you're gone now.—You treated me badly—that was wicked of you—but sleep peacefully, Liliom—you bad, bad boy, you—I love you—I never told you before—I was ashamed—but now I've told you—I love you. Liliom—sleep—my boy—sleep. [*She rises, gets a Bible, sits down near the candle and reads softly to herself, so that, not the words, but an inarticulate murmur is heard. The* CARPENTER *enters at back.*]

CARPENTER

[*Stands near the door; in the dimness of the room he can scarcely be seen.*] Miss Julie——

JULIE

[*Without alarm.*] Who is that?

CARPENTER

[*Very slowly.*] The carpenter.

JULIE

What does the carpenter want?

CARPENTER

Can I be of help to you in any way? Shall I stay here with you?

JULIE

[*Gratefully, but firmly.*] Don't stay, carpenter.

CARPENTER

Shall I come back tomorrow?

JULIE

Not tomorrow, either.

CARPENTER

Don't be offended, Miss Julie, but I'd like to know—you see, I'm not a young man any more—I have two children—and if I'm to come back any more—I'd like to know—if there's any use——

JULIE

No use, carpenter.

CARPENTER

[*As he exits.*] God be with you. [JULIE *resumes her reading.* FICSUR *enters, slinks furtively sideways to the stretcher, looks at* LILIOM, *shakes his head.* JULIE *looks up from her reading.* FICSUR *takes fright, slinks away from the stretcher, sits down at right, biting his nails.* JULIE *rises.* FICSUR *rises, too, and looks at her half fearfully. With her piercing glance upon him he slinks to the doorway at back, where he pauses and speaks.*]

FICSUR

The old woman asked me to tell you that coffee is ready, and you are to come in. [JULIE *goes to the kitchen door.* FICSUR *withdraws until she has closed the door behind her. Then he reappears in the doorway, stands on tiptoes, looks at* LILIOM, *then exits. Now the body lies alone. After a brief silence music is heard, distant at first, but gradually coming nearer. It is very much like the music of the carousel, but slower, graver, more exalted. The melody, too, is the same, yet the tempo is altered and contrapuntal measures of the thieves' song are intertwined in it. Two men in black, with heavy sticks, soft black hats and black gloves, appear in the doorway at back and stride slowly into the room. Their faces are beardless, marble white, grave and benign. One stops in front of the stretcher, the other a pace to the right. From above a dim violet light illuminates their faces.*]

THE FIRST

[*To* LILIOM.] Rise and come with us.

THE SECOND

[*Politely.*] You're under arrest.

THE FIRST

[*Somewhat louder, but always in a gentle, low, resonant voice.*] Do you hear? Rise. Don't you hear?

THE SECOND

We are the police.

THE FIRST

[*Bends down, touches* LILIOM'S *shoulder.*] Get up and come with us. [LILIOM *slowly sits up.*]

THE SECOND

Come along.

THE FIRST

[*Paternally.*] These people suppose that when they die all their difficulties are solved for them.

THE SECOND

[*Raising his voice sternly.*] That simply by thrusting a knife in your heart and making it stop beating you can leave your wife behind with a child in her womb——

THE FIRST

It is not as simple as that.

THE SECOND

Such things are not settled so easily.

THE FIRST

Come along. You will have to give an account of yourself. [*As both bow their heads, he continues softly.*] We are God's police. [*An expression of glad relief lights upon* LILIOM's *face. He rises from the stretcher.*] Come.

THE SECOND

You mortals don't get off quite as easy as that.

THE FIRST

[*Softly.*] Come. [LILIOM *starts to walk ahead of them, then stops and looks at them.*] The end is not as abrupt as that. Your name is still spoken. Your face is still remembered. And what you said, and what you did, and what you failed to do—these are still remembered. Remembered, too, are the manner of your glance, the ring of your voice, the clasp of your hand and how your step sounded—as long as one is left who remembers you, so long is the matter unended. Before the end there is much to be undone. Until you are quite forgotten, my son, you will not be finished with the earth—even though you *are* dead.

The Second

[*Very gently.*] Come. [*The music begins again. All three exit at back,* Liliom *leading, the others following. The stage is empty and quite dark save for the candle which burns by the stretcher, on which, in the shadows, the covers are so arranged that one cannot quite be sure that a body is not still lying. The music dies out in the distance as if it had followed* Liliom *and the two* Policemen. *The candle flickers and goes out. There is a brief interval of silence and total darkness before*

The Curtain Falls

The Richly Dressed Man

[*Points to the* Poorly Dressed Man.] So's he. [*Introducing himself.*] My name is Reich.

The Poorly Dressed Man

[*Whispers, too.*] My name is Stephen Kadar. [Liliom *only looks at them.*]

The Poorly Dressed Man

And you? What's your name?

Liliom

None of your business. [*Both move a bit away from him.*]

The Poorly Dressed Man

I did it by jumping out of a window.

The Richly Dressed Man

I did it with a pistol—and you?

Liliom

With a knife. [*They move a bit further away from him.*]

The Richly Dressed Man

A pistol is cleaner.

Liliom

If I had the price of a pistol——

The Second

Silence!

[*The* Police Magistrate *enters. He has a long white beard, is bald, but only in profile can be seen on his head a single tuft of snow-white hair. The* Guard *reënters behind him and sits on the bench with the dead men. As the* Magistrate *enters, all rise, except* Liliom, *who remains surlily seated. When the* Magistrate *sits down, so do the others.*]

The Guard

Yesterday's cases, your honor. The numbers are entered in the docket.

The Magistrate

Number 16,472.

The First

[*Looks in his notebook, beckons the* Richly Dressed Man.] Stand up, please. [The Richly Dressed Man *rises.*]

The Magistrate

Your name?

SCENE SIX

SCENE—*In the Beyond. A whitewashed courtroom. There is a green-topped table; behind it a bench. Back Center is a door with a bell over it. Next to this door is a window through which can be seen a vista of rose-tinted clouds.*

Down right there is a grated iron door. Down left another door.

Two men are on the bench when the curtain rises. One is richly, the other poorly dressed.

From a great distance is heard a fanfare of trumpets playing the refrain of the thieves' song in slow, altered tempo.

Passing the window at back appear LILIOM *and the two policemen.*

The bell rings.

An old guard enters at right. He is bald and has a long white beard. He wears the conventional police uniform.

He goes to the door at back, opens it, exchanges silent greetings with the two policemen and closes the door again.

LILIOM *looks wonderingly around.*

The First

[*To the old guard.*] Announce us. [*The guard exits at left.*]

Liliom

Is this it?

The Second

Yes, my son.

Liliom

This is the police court?

The Second

Yes, my son. The part for suicide cases.

Liliom

And what happens here?

The First

Here justice is done. Sit down. [Liliom *sits next to the two men. The two policemen stand silent near the table.*]

The Richly Dressed Man

[*Whispers.*] Suicide, too?

Liliom

Yes.

THE RICHLY DRESSED MAN

Doctor Reich.

THE MAGISTRATE

Age?

THE RICHLY DRESSED MAN

Forty-two, married, Jew.

THE MAGISTRATE

[*With a gesture of dismissal.*] Religion does not interest us here—why did you kill yourself?

THE RICHLY DRESSED MAN

On account of debts.

THE MAGISTRATE

What good did you do on earth?

THE RICHLY DRESSED MAN

I was a lawyer——

THE MAGISTRATE

[*Coughs significantly.*] Yes—we'll discuss that later. For the present I shall only ask you: Would you like to go back to earth once more before sunrise? I advise you that you have the right to go if you choose. Do you understand?

THE RICHLY DRESSED MAN

Yes, sir.

THE MAGISTRATE

He who takes his life is apt, in his haste and his excitement, to forget something. Is there anything important down there you have left undone? Something to tell someone? Something to undo?

THE RICHLY DRESSED MAN

My debts——

THE MAGISTRATE

They do not matter here. Here we are concerned only with the affairs of the soul.

THE RICHLY DRESSED MAN

Then—if you please—when I left—the house—my youngest son, Oscar—was asleep. I didn't trust myself to wake him—and bid him good-bye. I would have liked—to kiss him good-bye.

THE MAGISTRATE

[*To* THE SECOND.] You will take Dr. Reich back and let him kiss his son Oscar.

THE SECOND

Come with me, please.

The Richly Dressed Man

[*To* The Magistrate.] I thank you. [*He bows and exits at back with* The Second.]

The Magistrate

[*After making an entry in the docket.*] Number 16,473.

The First

[*Looks in his notebook, then beckons* Liliom.] Stand up.

Liliom

You said *please* to him. [*He rises.*]

The Magistrate

Your name?

Liliom

Liliom.

The Magistrate

Isn't that your nickname?

Liliom

Yes.

The Magistrate

What is your right name?

Liliom

Andreas.

The Magistrate

And your last name?

Liliom

Zavocki—after my mother.

The Magistrate

Your age?

Liliom

Twenty-four.

The Magistrate

What good did *you* do on earth? [Liliom *is silent*.] Why did you take your life? [Liliom *does not answer*. The Magistrate *addresses* The First.] Take that knife away from him. [The First *does so*.] It will be returned to you, if you go back to earth.

Liliom

Do I go back to earth again?

The Magistrate

Just answer my questions.

Liliom

I wasn't answering then, I was asking if——

The Magistrate

You don't ask questions here. You only answer. Only answer, Andreas Zavocki! I ask you whether

LILIOM 155

there is anything on earth you neglected to accomplish? Anything down there you would like to do?

LILIOM

Yes.

THE MAGISTRATE

What is it?

LILIOM

I'd like to break Ficsur's head for him.

THE MAGISTRATE

Punishment is our office. Is there nothing else on earth you'd like to do?

LILIOM

I don't know—I guess, as long as I'm here, I'll not go back.

THE MAGISTRATE

[*To* THE FIRST.] Note that. He waives his right. [LILIOM *starts back to the bench.*] Stay where you are. You are aware that you left your wife without food or shelter?

LILIOM

Yes.

THE MAGISTRATE

Don't you regret it?

LILIOM
No.

THE MAGISTRATE
You are aware that your wife is pregnant, and that in six months a child will be born?

LILIOM
I know.

THE MAGISTRATE
And that the child, too, will be without food or shelter? Do you regret that?

LILIOM
As long as I won't be there, what's it got to do with me?

THE MAGISTRATE
Don't try to deceive us, Andreas Zavocki. We see through you as through a pane of glass.

LILIOM
If you see so much, what do you want to ask me for? Why don't you let me rest—in peace?

THE MAGISTRATE
First you must earn your rest.

LILIOM
I want—only—to sleep.

The Magistrate

Your obstinacy won't help you. Here patience is endless as time. We can wait.

Liliom

Can I ask something—I'd like to know—if Your Honor will tell me—whether the baby will be a boy or a girl.

The Magistrate

You shall see that for yourself.

Liliom

[*Excitedly.*] I'll see the baby?

The Magistrate

When you do it won't be a baby any more. But we haven't reached that question yet.

Liliom

I'll see it?

The Magistrate

Again I ask you: Do you not regret that you deserted your wife and child; that you were a bad husband, a bad father?

Liliom

A bad husband?

The Magistrate

Yes.

Liliom

And a bad father?

The Magistrate

That, too.

Liliom

I couldn't get work—and I couldn't bear to see Julie—all the time—all the time——

The Magistrate

Weeping! Why are you ashamed to say it? You couldn't bear to see her weeping. Why are you afraid of that word? And why are you ashamed that you loved her?

Liliom

[*Shrugs his shoulders.*] Who's ashamed? But I couldn't bear to see her—and that's why I was bad to her. You see, it wouldn't do to go back to the carousel—and Ficsur came along with his talk about—that other thing—and all of a sudden it happened, I don't know how. The police and the Jew with the pistol—and there I stood—and I'd lost the money playing cards—and I didn't want to be put in prison. [*Demanding justification.*] Maybe I was wrong not to go out and steal when there was nothing to eat in the house? Should I have gone out to steal for Julie?

The Magistrate

[*Emphatically.*] Yes.

Liliom

[*After an astounded pause.*] The police down there never said that.

The Magistrate

You beat that poor, frail girl; you beat her because she loved you. How could you do that?

Liliom

We argued with each other—she said this and I said that—and because she was right I couldn't answer her—and I got mad—and the anger rose up in me—until it reached here [*points to his throat*] and then I beat her.

The Magistrate

Are you sorry?

Liliom

[*Shakes his head, but cannot utter the word "no"; continues softly.*] When I touched her slender throat—then—if you like—you might say—— [*Falters, looks embarrassed at* The Magistrate.]

The Magistrate

[*Confidently expectant.*] Are you sorry?

LILIOM

[*With a stare.*] I'm not sorry for anything.

THE MAGISTRATE

Liliom, Liliom, it will be difficult to help you.

LILIOM

I'm not asking any help.

THE MAGISTRATE

You were offered employment as a caretaker on Arader Street. [*To* THE FIRST.] Where is that entered?

THE FIRST

In the small docket. [*Hands him the open book.* THE MAGISTRATE *looks in it.*]

THE MAGISTRATE

Rooms, kitchen, quarterly wages, the privilege of keeping poultry. Why didn't you accept it?

LILIOM

I'm not a caretaker. I'm no good at caretaking. To be a caretaker——you have to be a caretaker——

THE MAGISTRATE

If I said to you now: Liliom, go back on your stretcher. Tomorrow morning you will arise alive and well again. Would you be a caretaker then?

Liliom

No.

The Magistrate

Why not?

Liliom

Because—because that's just why I died.

The Magistrate

That is not true, my son. You died because you loved little Julie and the child she is bearing under her heart.

Liliom

No.

The Magistrate

Look me in the eye.

Liliom

[*Looks him in the eye.*] No.

The Magistrate

[*Stroking his beard.*] Liliom, Liliom, if it were not for our Heavenly patience—— Go back to your seat. Number 16,474.

The First

[*Looks in his note book.*] Stephan Kadar. [The Poorly Dressed Man *rises.*]

THE MAGISTRAT

You came out today?

THE POORLY DRESSED MAN

Today.

THE MAGISTRATE

[*Indicating the crimson sea of clouds.*] How long were you in there?

THE POORLY DRESSED MAN

Thirteen years.

THE MAGISTRATE

Officer, you went to earth with him?

THE FIRST

Yes, sir.

THE MAGISTRATE

Stephan Kadar, after thirteen years of purification by fire you returned to earth to give proof that your soul had been burned clean. What good deed did you perform?

THE POORLY DRESSED MAN

When I came to the village and looked in the window of our cottage I saw my poor little orphans sleeping peacefully. But it was raining and the rain beat into the room through a hole in the roof.

So I went and fixed the roof so it wouldn't rain in any more. My hammering woke them up and they were afraid. But their mother came in to them and comforted them. She said to them: "Don't cry! It's your poor, dear father hammering up there. He's come back from the other world to fix the roof for us."

THE MAGISTRATE

Officer?

THE FIRST

That's what happened.

THE MAGISTRATE

Stephan Kadar, you have done a good deed. What you did will be written in books to gladden the hearts of children who read them. [*Indicates the door at left.*] The door is open to you. The eternal light awaits you. [THE FIRST *escorts the* POORLY DRESSED MAN *out at left with great deference.*] Liliom! [LILIOM *rises.*] You have heard?

LILIOM

Yes.

THE MAGISTRATE

When this man first appeared before us he was as stubborn as you. But now he has purified himself and withstood the test. He has done a good deed.

LILIOM

What's he done, anyhow? Any roofer can fix a roof. It's much harder to be a barker in an amusement park.

THE MAGISTRATE

Liliom, you shall remain for sixteen years in the crimson fire until your child is full grown. By that time your pride and your stubbornness will have been burnt out of you. And when your daughter——

LILIOM

My daughter!

THE MAGISTRATE

When your daughter has reached the age of sixteen—— [LILIOM *bows his head, covers his eyes with his hands, and to keep from weeping laughs defiantly, sadly.*]

THE MAGISTRATE

When your daughter has reached the age of sixteen you will be sent for one day back to earth.

LILIOM

Me?

THE MAGISTRATE

Yes—just as you may have read in the legends of how the dead reappear on earth for a time.

Liliom

I never believed them.

The Magistrate

Now you see they are true. You will go back to earth one day to show how far the purification of your soul has progressed.

Liliom

Then I must show what I can do—like when you apply for a job—as a coachman?

The Magistrate

Yes—it is a test.

Liliom

And will I be told what I have to do?

The Magistrate

No.

Liliom

How will I know, then?

The Magistrate

You must decide that for yourself. That's what you burn sixteen years for. And if you do something good, something splendid for your child, then——

LILIOM

[*Laughs sadly.*] Then? [*All stand up and bow their heads reverently. There is a pause.*] Then?

THE MAGISTRATE

Now I'll bid you farewell, Liliom. Sixteen years and a day shall pass before I see you again. When you have returned from earth you will come up before me again. Take heed and think well of some good deed to do for your child. On that will depend which door shall be opened to you up here. Now go, Liliom. [*He exits at left.* THE GUARD *stands at attention. There is a pause.*]

THE FIRST

[*Approaches* LILIOM.] Come along, my son. [*He goes to the door at right; pulls open the bolt and waits.*]

LILIOM

[*To the old* GUARD, *softly.*] Say, officer.

THE GUARD

What do you want?

LILIOM

Please—can I get—have you got——?

THE GUARD

What?

LILIOM

[*Whispers.*] A cigarette? [*The old* GUARD *stares at him, goes a few paces to the left, shakes his head disapprovingly. Then his expression softens. He takes a cigarette from his pocket and, crossing to* LILIOM—*who has gone over to the door at right—gives him the cigarette.* THE FIRST *throws open the door. An intense rose-colored light streams in. The glow of it is so strong that it blinds* LILIOM *and he takes a step backward and bows his head and covers his eyes with his hand before he steps forward into the light.*]

THE CURTAIN FALLS

SCENE SEVEN

SCENE—*Sixteen years later. A small, tumble-down house on a bare, unenclosed plot of ground. Before the house is a tiny garden enclosed by a hip-high hedge.*

At back a wooden fence crosses the stage; in the center of it is a door large enough to admit a wagon. Beyond the fence is a view of a suburban street which blends into a broad vista of tilled fields.

It is a bright Sunday in Spring.

In the garden a table for two is laid.

JULIE, her daughter LOUISE, WOLF and MARIE are discovered in the garden. WOLF is prosperously dressed, MARIE somewhat elaborately, with a huge hat.

JULIE

You could stay for lunch.

MARIE

Impossible, dear. Since he became the proprietor of the Café Sorrento, Wolf simply has to be there all the time.

JULIE

But you needn't stay there all day, too.

MARIE

Oh, yes. I sit near the cashier's cage, read the papers, keep an eye on the waiters and drink in the bustle and excitement of the great city.

JULIE

And what about the children?

MARIE

You know what modern families are like. Parents scarcely ever see their children these days. The four girls are with their governess, the three boys with their tutor.

LOUISE

Auntie, dear, do stay and eat with us.

MARIE

[*Importantly.*] Impossible today, dear child, impossible. Perhaps some other time. Come, Mr. Beifeld.

JULIE

Since when do you call your husband mister?

WOLF

I'd rather she did, dear lady. When we used to be very familiar we quarreled all the time. Now we are formal with each other and get along like society folk. I kiss your hand, dear lady.

JULIE

Good-bye, Wolf.

MARIE

Adieu, my dear. [*They embrace.*] Adieu, my dear child.

LOUISE

Good-bye, Aunt Marie. Good-bye, Uncle Wolf. [WOLF *and* MARIE *exit.*]

JULIE

You can get the soup now, Louise dear. [LOUISE *goes into the house and reënters with the soup. They sit at the table.*]

LOUISE

Mother, is it true we're not going to work at the jute factory any more?

JULIE

Yes, dear.

LOUISE

Where then?

JULIE

Uncle Wolf has gotten us a place in a big establishment where they make all kinds of fittings for cafés. We're to make big curtains, you know, the kind they hang in the windows, with lettering on them.

LOUISE

It'll be nicer there than at the jute factory.

JULIE

Yes, dear. The work isn't as dirty and pays better, too. A poor widow like your mother is lucky to get it. [*They eat.* LILIOM *and the two* HEAVENLY POLICEMEN *appear in the big doorway at back. The* POLICEMEN *pass slowly by.* LILIOM *stands there alone a moment, then comes slowly down and pauses at the opening of the hedge. He is dressed as he was on the day of his death. He is very pale, but otherwise unaltered.* JULIE, *at the table, has her back to him.* LOUISE *sits facing the audience.*

LILIOM

Good day.

LOUISE

Good day.

JULIE

Another beggar! What is it you want, my poor man?

LILIOM

Nothing.

JULIE

We have no money to give, but if you care for a plate of soup—— [LOUISE *goes into the house.*] Have you come far today?

LILIOM

Yes—very far.

JULIE

Are you tired?

LILIOM

Very tired.

JULIE

Over there at the gate is a stone. Sit down and rest. My daughter is bringing you the soup. [LOUISE *comes out of the house.*]

LILIOM

Is that your daughter?

JULIE

Yes.

LILIOM

[*To* LOUISE.] You are the daughter?

LOUISE

Yes, sir.

LILIOM

A fine, healthy girl. [*Takes the soup plate from her with one hand, while with the other he touches her arm.* LOUISE *draws back quickly.*]

LOUISE

[*Crosses to* JULIE.] Mother!

JULIE

What, my child?

LOUISE

The man tried to take me by the arm.

JULIE

Nonsense! You only imagined it, dear. The poor, hungry man has other things to think about than fooling with young girls. Sit down and eat your soup. [*They eat.*]

LILIOM

[*Eats, too, but keeps looking at them.*] You work at the factory, eh?

JULIE

Yes.

LILIOM

Your daughter, too?

LOUISE

Yes.

LILIOM

And your husband?

JULIE

[*After a pause.*] I have no husband. I'm a widow.

LILIOM

A widow?

JULIE

Yes.

LILIOM

Your husband—I suppose he's been dead a long time. [JULIE *does not answer.*] I say—has your husband been dead a long time?

JULIE

A long time.

LILIOM

What did he die of? [JULIE *is silent.*]

LOUISE

No one knows. He went to America to work and he died there—in the hospital. Poor father, I never knew him.

LILIOM

He went to America?

LOUISE

Yes, before I was born.

LILIOM

To America?

JULIE

Why do you ask so many questions? Did you know him, perhaps?

LILIOM

[*Puts the plate down.*] Heaven knows! I've known so many people. Maybe I knew him, too.

JULIE

Well, if you knew him, leave him and us in peace with your questions. He went to America and died there. That's all there is to tell.

LILIOM

All right. All right. Don't be angry with me. I didn't mean any harm. [*There is a pause.*]

LOUISE

My father was a very handsome man.

JULIE

Don't talk so much.

LOUISE

Did I say anything——?

LILIOM

Surely the little orphan can say that about her father.

LOUISE

My father could juggle so beautifully with three ivory balls that people used to advise him to go on the stage.

JULIE

Who told you that?

LOUISE

Uncle Wolf.

LILIOM

Who is that?

LOUISE

Mr. Wolf Beifeld, who owns the Café Sorrento.

LILIOM

The one who used to be a porter?

JULIE

[*Astonished.*] Do you know him, too? It seems that you know all Budapest.

LILIOM

Wolf Beifeld is a long way from being all Budapest. But I do know a lot of people. Why shouldn't I know Wolf Beifeld?

LOUISE

He was a friend of my father.

JULIE

He was not his friend. No one was.

LILIOM

You speak of your husband so sternly.

JULIE

What's that to you? Doesn't it suit you? I can speak of my husband any way I like. It's nobody's business but mine.

LILIOM

Certainly, certainly—it's your own business. [*Takes up his soup plate again. All three eat.*]

LOUISE

[*To* JULIE.] Perhaps he knew father, too.

JULIE

Ask him, if you like.

LOUISE

[*Crosses to* LILIOM. *He stands up.*] Did you know my father? [LILIOM *nods.* LOUISE *addresses her mother.*] Yes, he knew him.

JULIE

[*Rises.*] You knew Andreas Zavocky?

LILIOM

Liliom? Yes.

LOUISE

Was he really a very handsome man?

LILIOM

I wouldn't exactly say handsome.

LOUISE

[*Confidently.*] But he was an awfully good man, wasn't he?

LILIOM

He wasn't so good, either. As far as I know he was what they called a clown, a barker in a carousel.

LOUISE

[*Pleased.*] Did he tell funny jokes?

LILIOM

Lots of 'em. And he sang funny songs, too.

LOUISE

In the carousel?

LILIOM

Yes—but he was something of a bully, too. He'd fight anyone. He even hit your dear little mother.

JULIE

That's a lie.

LILIOM

It's true.

JULIE

Aren't you ashamed to tell the child such awful things about her father? Get out of here, you shameless liar. Eats our soup and our bread and has the impudence to slander our dead!

LILIOM

I didn't mean—I——

JULIE

What right have you to tell lies to the child? Take that plate, Louise, and let him be on his way. If he wasn't such a hungry-looking beggar, I'd put him out myself. [LOUISE *takes the plate out of his hand.*]

LILIOM

So he didn't hit you?

JULIE

No, never. He was always good to me.

LOUISE

[*Whispers.*] Did he tell funny stories, too?

LILIOM

Yes, and *such* funny ones.

Julie

Don't speak to him any more.   In God's name, go.

Louise

In God's name.   [Julie *resumes her seat at the table and eats.*]

Liliom

If you please, Miss—I have a pack of cards in my pocket. And if you like, I'll show you some tricks that'll make you split your sides laughing. [Louise *holds* Liliom's *plate in her left hand. With her right she reaches out and holds the garden gate shut.*] Let me in, just a little way, Miss, and I'll do the tricks for you.

Louise

Go, in God's name, and let us be.   Why are you making those ugly faces?

Liliom

Don't chase me away, Miss; let me come in for just a minute—just for a minute—just long enough to let me show you something pretty, something wonderful. [*Opens the gate.*] Miss, I've something to give you. [*Takes from his pocket a big red handkerchief in which is wrapped a glittering star from Heaven. He looks furtively about him to make sure that the* Police *are not watching.*]

LOUISE

What's that?

LILIOM

Pst! A star! [*With a gesture he indicates that he has stolen it out of the sky.*]

JULIE

[*Sternly.*] Don't take anything from him. He's probably stolen it somewhere. [*To* LILIOM.] In God's name, be off with you.

LOUISE

Yes, be off with you. Be off. [*She slams the gate.*]

LILIOM

Miss—please, Miss—I've got to do something good—or—do something good—a good deed——

LOUISE

[*Pointing with her right hand.*] That's the way out.

LILIOM

Miss——

LOUISE

Get out!

LILIOM

Miss! [*Looks up at her suddenly and slaps her extended hand, so that the slap resounds loudly.*]

LOUISE

Mother! [*Looks dazedly at* LILIOM, *who bows his head dismayed, forlorn.* JULIE *rises and looks at* LILIOM *in astonishment. There is a long pause.*]

JULIE

[*Comes over to them slowly.*] What's the matter here?

LOUISE

[*Bewildered, does not take her eyes off* LILIOM.] Mother—the man—he hit me—on the hand—hard—I heard the sound of it—but it didn't hurt—mother—it didn't hurt—it was like a caress—as if he had just touched my hand tenderly. [*She hides behind* JULIE. LILIOM *sulkily raises his head and looks at* JULIE.]

JULIE

[*Softly.*] Go, my child. Go into the house. Go.

LOUISE

[*Going.*] But mother—I'm afraid—it sounded so loud—— [*Weepingly.*] And it didn't hurt at all—just as if he'd—kissed my hand instead—mother! [*She hides her face.*]

JULIE

Go in, my child, go in. [LOUISE *goes slowly into the house.* JULIE *watches her until she has disappeared, then turns slowly to* LILIOM.]

JULIE

You struck my child.

LILIOM

Yes—I struck her.

JULIE

Is that what you came for, to strike my child?

LILIOM

No—I didn't come for that—but I did strike her—and now I'm going back.

JULIE

In the name of the Lord Jesus, who are you?

LILIOM

[*Simply.*] A poor, tired beggar who came a long way and who was hungry. And I took your soup and bread and I struck your child. Are you angry with me?

JULIE

[*Her hand on her heart; fearfully, wonderingly.*] Jesus protect me—I don't understand it—I'm *not* angry—not angry at all—— [*LILIOM goes to the doorway and leans against the doorpost, his back to the audience. JULIE goes to the table and sits.*]

JULIE

Louise! [LOUISE *comes out of the house.*] Sit down, dear, we'll finish eating.

LOUISE

Has he gone?

JULIE

Yes. [*They are both seated at the table.* LOUISE, *her head in her hands, is staring into space.*] Why don't you eat, dear?

LOUISE

What has happened, mother?

JULIE

Nothing, my child. [*The* HEAVENLY POLICEMEN *appear outside.* LILIOM *walks slowly off at left. The* FIRST POLICEMAN *makes a deploring gesture. Both shake their heads deploringly and follow* LILIOM *slowly off at left.*]

LOUISE

Mother, dear, why won't you tell me?

JULIE

What is there to tell you, child? Nothing has happened. We were peacefully eating, and a beggar came who talked of bygone days, and then I thought of your father.

LOUISE

My father?

JULIE

Your father—Liliom. [*There is a pause.*]

LOUISE

Mother—tell me—has it ever happened to you—has anyone ever hit you—without hurting you in the least?

JULIE

Yes, my child. It has happened to me, too. [*There is a pause.*]

LOUISE

Is it possible for someone to hit you—hard like that—real loud and hard—and not hurt you at all?

JULIE

It is possible, dear—that someone may beat you and beat you and beat you,—and not hurt you at all.—— [*There is a pause. Nearby an organ-grinder has stopped. The music of his organ begins.*]

THE CURTAIN FALLS

BOOK JUNGLE

Bringing Classics to Life

www.bookjungle.com email: sales@bookjungle.com fax: 630-214-0564 mail: Book Jungle PO Box 2226 Champaign, IL 61825

The Two Babylons
Alexander Hislop QTY

You may be surprised to learn that many traditions of Roman Catholicism in fact don't come from Christ's teachings but from an ancient Babylonian "Mystery" religion that was centered on Nimrod, his wife Semiramis, and a child Tammuz. This book shows how this ancient religion transformed itself as it incorporated Christ into its teachings....

Religion/History Pages: 358
ISBN: *1-59462-010-5* MSRP **$22.95**

The Go-Getter
Kyne B. Peter QTY

The Go Getter is the story of William Peck. He was a war veteran and amputee who will not be refused what he wants. Peck not only fights to find employment but continually proves himself more than competent at the many difficult test that are throw his way in the course of his early days with the Ricks Lumber Company...

Business/Self Help/Inspirational Pages: 68
ISBN: *1-59462-186-1* MSRP **$8.95**

The Power Of Concentration
Theron Q. Dumont

It is of the utmost value to learn how to concentrate. To make the greatest success of anything you must be able to concentrate your entire thought upon the idea you are working on. The person that is able to concentrate utilizes all constructive thoughts and shuts out all destructive ones...

Self Help/Inspirational Pages: 196
ISBN: *1-59462-141-1* MSRP **$14.95**

Self Mastery
Emile Coue

Emile Coue came up with novel way to improve the lives of people. He was a pharmacist by trade and often saw ailing people. This lead him to develop autosuggestion, a form of self-hypnosis. At the time his theories weren't popular but over the years evidence is mounting that he was indeed right all along...

New Age/Self Help Pages: 98
ISBN: *1-59462-189-6* MSRP **$7.95**

Rightly Dividing The Word
Clarence Larkin

The "Fundamental Doctrines" of the Christian Faith are clearly outlined in numerous books on Theology, but they are not available to the average reader and were mainly written for students. The Author has made it the work of his ministry to preach the "Fundamental Doctrines." To this end he has aimed to express them in the simplest and clearest manner...

Religion Pages: 352
ISBN: *1-59462-334-1* MSRP **$23.45**

The Awful Disclosures Of Maria Monk

"I cannot banish the scenes and characters of this book from my memory. To me it can never appear like an amusing fable, or lose its interest and importance. The story is one which is continually before me, and must return fresh to my mind with painful emotions as long as I live.."

Religion Pages: 232
ISBN: *1-59462-160-8* MSRP **$17.95**

The Law of Psychic Phenomena
Thomson Jay Hudson

I do not expect this book to stand upon its literary merits; for if it is unsound in principle, felicity of diction cannot save it, and if sound, homeliness of expression cannot destroy it. My primary object in offering it to the public is to assist in bringing Psychology within the domain of the exact sciences. That this has never been accomplished..."

New Age Pages: 420
ISBN: *1-59462-124-1* MSRP **$29.95**

As a Man Thinketh
James Allen

"This little volume (the result of meditation and experience) is not intended as an exhaustive treatise on the much-written-upon subject of the power of thought. It is suggestive rather than explanatory, its object being to stimulate men and women to the discovery and perception of the truth that by virtue of the thoughts which they choose and encourage..."

Inspirational/Self Help Pages: 80
ISBN: *1-59462-231-0* MSRP **$9.45**

Beautiful Joe
Marshall Saunders

When Marshall visited the Moore family in 1892, she discovered Joe, a dog they had nursed back to health from his previous abusive home to live a happy life. So moved was she, that she wrote this classic masterpiece which won accolades and was recognized as a heartwarming symbol for humane animal treatment...

Fiction Pages: 256
ISBN: *1-59462-261-2* MSRP **$18.45**

The Enchanted April
Elizabeth Von Arnim

It began in a woman's club in London on a February afternoon, an uncomfortable club, and a miserable afternoon when Mrs. Wilkins, who had come down from Hampstead to shop and had lunched at her club, took up The Times from the table in the smoking-room...

Fiction Pages: 368
ISBN: *1-59462-150-0* MSRP **$23.45**

The Codes Of Hammurabi And Moses - W. W. Davies

The discovery of the Hammurabi Code is one of the greatest achievements of archaeology, and is of paramount interest, not only to the student of the Bible, but also to all those interested in ancient history...

Religion Pages: 132
ISBN: *1-59462-338-4* MSRP **$12.95**

Holland - The History Of Netherlands
Thomas Colley Grattan

Thomas Grattan was a prestigious writer from Dublin who served as British Consul to the US. Among his works is an authoritative look at the history of Holland. A colorful and interesting look at history....

History/Politics Pages: 408
ISBN: *1-59462-137-3* MSRP **$26.95**

The Thirty-Six Dramatic Situations
Georges Polti

An incredibly useful guide for aspiring authors and playwrights. This volume categorizes every dramatic situation which could occur in a story and describes them in a list of 36 situations. A great aid to help inspire or formalize the creative writing process...

Self Help/Reference Pages: 204
ISBN: *1-59462-134-9* MSRP **$15.95**

A Concise Dictionary of Middle English
A. L. Mayhew
Walter W. Skeat

The present work is intended to meet, in some measure, the requirements of those who wish to make some study of Middle-English, and who find a difficulty in obtaining such assistance as will enable them to find out the meanings and etymologies of the words most essential to their purpose...

Reference/History Pages: 332
ISBN: *1-59462-119-5* MSRP **$29.95**

www.bookjungle.com email: sales@bookjungle.com fax: 630-214-0564 mail: Book Jungle PO Box 2226 Champaign, IL 61825

BOOK JUNGLE
Bringing Classics to Life

www.bookjungle.com email: sales@bookjungle.com fax: 630-214-0564 mail: Book Jungle PO Box 2226 Champaign, IL 61825

The Witch-Cult in Western Europe
Margaret Murray QTY

The mass of existing material on this subject is so great that I have not attempted to make a survey of the whole of European "Witchcraft" but have confined myself to an intensive study of the cult in Great Britain. In order, however, to obtain a clearer understanding of the ritual and beliefs I have had recourse to French and Flemish sources...

Occult Pages:308
ISBN: *1-59462-126-8* MSRP *$22.45*

Philosophy Of Natural Therapeutics
Henry Lindlahr QTY

We invite the earnest cooperation in this great work of all those who have awakened to the necessity for more rational living and for radical reform in healing methods...

Health/Philosophy/Self Help Pages:552
ISBN: *1-59462-132-2* MSRP *$34.95*

The Science Of Psychic Healing
Yogi Ramacharaka

This book is not a book of theories it deals with facts. Its author regards the best of theories as but working hypotheses to be used only until better ones present themselves. The "fact" is the principal thing the essential thing to uncover which the tool, theory, is used...

New Age/Health Pages:180
ISBN: *1-59462-140-3* MSRP *$13.95*

A Message to Garcia
Elbert Hubbard

This literary trifle, A Message to Garcia, was written one evening after supper, in a single hour. It was on the Twenty-second of February, Eighteen Hundred Ninety-nine, Washington's Birthday, and we were just going to press with the March Philistine...

New Age/Fiction Pages:92
ISBN: *1-59462-144-6* MSRP *$9.95*

Bible Myths
Thomas Doane

In pursuing the study of the Bible Myths, facts pertaining thereto, in a condensed form, seemed to be greatly needed, and nowhere to be found. Widely scattered through hundreds of ancient and modern volumes, most of the contents of this book may indeed be found; but any previous attempt to trace exclusively the myths and legends...

Religion/History Pages:644
ISBN: *1-59462-163-2* MSRP *$38.95*

The Book of Jasher
Alcuinus Flaccus Albinus

The Book of Jasher is an historical religious volume that many consider as a missing holy book from the Old Testament. Particularly studied by the Church of Later Day Saints and historians, it covers the history of the world from creation until the period of Judges in Israel. It's authenticity is bolstered due to a reference to the Book of Jasher in the Bible in Joshua 10:13

Religion/History Pages:276
ISBN: *1-59462-197-7* MSRP *$18.95*

Tertium Organum
P. D. Ouspensky

A truly mind expanding writing that combines science with mysticism with unprecedented elegance. He presents the world we live in as a multi dimensional world and time as a motion through this world. But this isn't a cold and purely analytical explanation but a masterful presentation filled with similes and analogies...

New Age Pages:356
ISBN: *1-59462-205-1* MSRP *$23.95*

The Titan
Theodore Dreiser

"When Frank Algernon Cowperwood emerged from the Eastern District Penitentiary, in Philadelphia he realized that the old life he had lived in that city since boyhood was ended. His youth was gone, and with it had been lost the great business prospects of his earlier manhood. He must begin again..."

Fiction Pages:564
ISBN: *1-59462-220-5* MSRP *$33.95*

Advance Course in Yogi Philosophy
Yogi Ramacharaka

"The twelve lessons forming this volume were originally issued in the shape of monthly lessons, known as "The Advanced Course in Yogi Philosophy and Oriental Occultism" during a period of twelve months beginning with October, 1904, and ending September, 1905."

Philosophy/Inspirational/Self Help Pages:340
ISBN: *1-59462-229-9* MSRP *$22.95*

Biblical Essays
J. B. Lightfoot

About one-third of the present volume has already seen the light. The opening essay "On the Internal Evidence for the Authenticity and Genuineness of St John's Gospel" was published in the "Expositor" in the early months of 1890, and has been reprinted since...

Religion/History Pages:480
ISBN: *1-59462-238-8* MSRP *$30.95*

Ambassador Morgenthau's Story
Henry Morgenthau

"By this time the American people have probably become convinced that the Germans deliberately planned the conquest of the world. Yet they hesitate to convict on circumstantial evidence and for this reason all eye witnesses to this, the greatest crime in modern history, should volunteer their testimony..."

History Pages:472
ISBN: *1-59462-244-2* MSRP *$29.95*

The Settlement Cook Book
Simon Kander

A legacy from the civil war, this book is a classic "American charity cookbook," which was used for fundraisers starting in Milwaukee. While it has transformed over the years, this printing provides great recipes from American history. Over two million copies have been sold. This volume contains a rich collection of recipes from noted chefs and hostesses of the turn of the century...

How-to Pages:472
ISBN: *1-59462-256-6* MSRP *$29.95*

The Aquarian Gospel of Jesus the Christ
Levi Dowling

A retelling of Jesus' story which tells us what happened during the twenty year gap left by the Bible's New Testament. It tells of his travels to the far-east where he studied with the masters and fought against the rigid caste system. This book has enjoyed a resurgence in modern America and provides spiritual insight with charm. Its influences can be seen throughout the Age of Aquarius...

Religion Pages:264
ISBN: *1-59462-321-X* MSRP *$18.95*

My Life and Work
Henry Ford

Henry Ford revolutionized the world with his implementation of mass production for the Model T automobile. Gain valuable business insight into his life and work with his own auto-biography... "We have only started on our development of our country we have not as yet, with all our talk of wonderful progress, done more than scratch the surface. The progress has been wonderful enough but..."

Biographies/History/Business Pages:300
ISBN: *1-59462-198-5* MSRP *$21.95*

---

www.bookjungle.com email: sales@bookjungle.com fax: 630-214-0564 mail: Book Jungle PO Box 2226 Champaign, IL 61825

BOOK JUNGLE

Bringing Classics to Life

www.bookjungle.com email: sales@bookjungle.com fax: 630-214-0564 mail: Book Jungle PO Box 2226 Champaign, IL 61825

QTY

☐	**The Rosicrucian Cosmo-Conception Mystic Christianity** by **Max Heindel** The Rosicrucian Cosmo-conception is not dogmatic, neither does it appeal to any other authority than the reason of the student. It is not controversial, but is sent forth in the hope that it may help to clear...	**ISBN: 1-59462-188-8** **$38.95** New Age/Religion Pages 646
☐	**Abandonment To Divine Providence** by **Jean-Pierre de Caussade** "The Rev. Jean Pierre de Caussade was one of the most remarkable spiritual writers of the Society of Jesus in France in the 18th Century. His death took place at Toulouse in 1751. His works have gone through many editions and have been republished...	**ISBN: 1-59462-228-0** **$25.95** Inspirational/Religion Pages 400
☐	**Mental Chemistry** by **Charles Haanel** Mental Chemistry allows the change of material conditions by combining and appropriately utilizing the power of the mind. Much like applied chemistry creates something new and unique out of careful combinations of chemicals the mastery of mental chemistry...	**ISBN: 1-59462-192-6** **$23.95** New Age Pages 354
☐	**The Letters of Robert Browning and Elizabeth Barret Barrett 1845-1846 vol II** by **Robert Browning** and **Elizabeth Barrett**	**ISBN: 1-59462-193-4** **$35.95** Biographies Pages 596
☐	**Gleanings In Genesis (volume I)** by **Arthur W. Pink** Appropriately has Genesis been termed "the seed plot of the Bible" for in it we have, in germ form, almost all of the great doctrines which are afterwards fully developed in the books of Scripture which follow...	**ISBN: 1-59462-130-6** **$27.45** Religion Inspirational Pages 420
☐	**The Master Key** by **L. W. de Laurence** In no branch of human knowledge has there been a more lively increase of the spirit of research during the past few years than in the study of Psychology, Concentration and Mental Discipline. The requests for authentic lessons in Thought Control, Mental Discipline and...	**ISBN: 1-59462-001-6** **$30.95** New Age/Business Pages 422
☐	**The Lesser Key Of Solomon Goetia** by **L. W. de Laurence** This translation of the first book of the "Lemegeton" which is now for the first time made accessible to students of Talismanic Magic was done, after careful collation and edition, from numerous Ancient Manuscripts in Hebrew, Latin, and French...	**ISBN: 1-59462-092-X** **$9.95** New Age/Occult Pages 92
☐	**Rubaiyat Of Omar Khayyam** by **Edward Fitzgerald** Edward Fitzgerald, whom the world has already learned, in spite of his own efforts to remain within the shadow of anonymity, to look upon as one of the rarest poets of the century, was born at Bredfield, in Suffolk, on the 31st of March, 1809. He was the third son of John Purcell...	**ISBN: 1-59462-332-5** **$13.95** Music Pages 172
☐	**Ancient Law** by **Henry Maine** The chief object of the following pages is to indicate some of the earliest ideas of mankind, as they are reflected in Ancient Law, and to point out the relation of those ideas to modern thought.	**ISBN: 1-59462-128-4** **$29.95** Religion/History Pages 452
☐	**Far-Away Stories** by **William J. Locke** "Good wine needs no bush, but a collection of mixed vintages does. And this book is just such a collection. Some of the stories I do not want to remain buried for ever in the museum files of dead magazine-numbers an author's not unpardonable vanity..."	**ISBN: 1-59462-129-2** **$19.45** Fiction Pages 272
☐	**Life of David Crockett** by **David Crockett** "Colonel David Crockett was one of the most remarkable men of the times in which he lived. Born in humble life, but gifted with a strong will, an indomitable courage, and unremitting perseverance...	**ISBN: 1-59462-250-7** **$27.45** Biographies/New Age Pages 424
☐	**Lip-Reading** by **Edward Nitchie** Edward B. Nitchie, founder of the New York School for the Hard of Hearing, now the Nitchie School of Lip-Reading, Inc, wrote "LIP-READING Principles and Practice". The development and perfecting of this meritorious work on lip-reading was an undertaking...	**ISBN: 1-59462-206-X** **$25.95** How-to Pages 400
☐	**A Handbook of Suggestive Therapeutics, Applied Hypnotism, Psychic Science** by **Henry Munro**	**ISBN: 1-59462-214-0** **$24.95** Health/New Age Health Self-help Pages 376
☐	**A Doll's House: and Two Other Plays** by **Henrik Ibsen** Henrik Ibsen created this classic when in revolutionary 1848 Rome. Introducing some striking concepts in playwriting for the realist genre, this play has been studied the world over.	**ISBN: 1-59462-112-8** **$19.95** Fiction/Classics/Plays 308
☐	**The Light of Asia** by **sir Edwin Arnold** In this poetic masterpiece, Edwin Arnold describes the life and teachings of Buddha. The man who was to become known as Buddha to the world was born as Prince Gautama of India but he rejected the worldly riches and abandoned the reigns of power when...	**ISBN: 1-59462-204-3** **$13.95** Religion/History Biographies Pages 170
☐	**The Complete Works of Guy de Maupassant** by **Guy de Maupassant** "For days and days, nights and nights, I had dreamed of that first kiss which was to consecrate our engagement, and I knew not on what spot I should put my lips..."	**ISBN: 1-59462-157-8** **$16.95** Fiction/Classics Pages 240
☐	**The Art of Cross-Examination** by **Francis L. Wellman** Written by a renowned trial lawyer, Wellman imparts his experience and uses case studies to explain how to use psychology to extract desired information through questioning.	**ISBN: 1-59462-309-0** **$26.95** How-to Science/Reference Pages 408
☐	**Answered or Unanswered?** by **Louisa Vaughan** Miracles of Faith in China	**ISBN: 1-59462-248-5** **$10.95** Religion Pages 112
☐	**The Edinburgh Lectures on Mental Science (1909)** by **Thomas** This book contains the substance of a course of lectures recently given by the writer in the Queen Street Hall, Edinburgh. Its purpose is to indicate the Natural Principles governing the relation between Mental Action and Material Conditions...	**ISBN: 1-59462-008-3** **$11.95** New Age/Psychology Pages 148
☐	**Ayesha** by **H. Rider Haggard** Verily and indeed it is the unexpected that happens! Probably if there was one person upon the earth from whom the Editor of this, and of a certain previous history, did not expect to hear again...	**ISBN: 1-59462-301-5** **$24.95** Classics Pages 380
☐	**Ayala's Angel** by **Anthony Trollope** The two girls were both pretty, but Lucy who was twenty-one who supposed to be simple and comparatively unattractive, whereas Ayala was credited, as her Bohemian romantic name might show, with poetic charm and a taste for romance. Ayala when her father died was nineteen...	**ISBN: 1-59462-352-X** **$29.95** Fiction Pages 484
☐	**The American Commonwealth** by **James Bryce** An interpretation of American democratic political theory. It examines political mechanics and society from the perspective of Scotsman James Bryce	**ISBN: 1-59462-286-8** **$34.45** Politics Pages 572
☐	**Stories of the Pilgrims** by **Margaret P. Pumphrey** This book explores pilgrims religious oppression in England as well as their escape to Holland and eventual crossing to America on the Mayflower, and their early days in New England...	**ISBN: 1-59462-116-0** **$17.95** History Pages 268

www.bookjungle.com email: sales@bookjungle.com fax: 630-214-0564 mail: Book Jungle PO Box 2226 Champaign, IL 61825

Bringing Classics to Life

BOOK JUNGLE

www.bookjungle.com email: sales@bookjungle.com fax: 630-214-0564 mail: Book Jungle PO Box 2226 Champaign, IL 61825

QTY

The Fasting Cure by **Sinclair Upton** ISBN: *1-59462-222-1* **$13.95**
In the Cosmopolitan Magazine for May, 1910, and in the Contemporary Review (London) for April, 1910, I published an article dealing with my experiences in fasting. I have written a great many magazine articles, but never one which attracted so much attention... *New Age/Self Help Health Pages 164*

Hebrew Astrology by **Sepharial** ISBN: *1-59462-308-2* **$13.45**
In these days of advanced thinking it is a matter of common observation that we have left many of the old landmarks behind and that we are now pressing forward to greater heights and to a wider horizon than that which represented the mind-content of our progenitors... *Astrology Pages 144*

Thought Vibration or The Law of Attraction in the Thought World ISBN: *1-59462-127-6* **$12.95**
by **William Walker Atkinson** *Psychology/Religion Pages 144*

Optimism by **Helen Keller** ISBN: *1-59462-108-X* **$15.95**
Helen Keller was blind, deaf, and mute since 19 months old, yet famously learned how to overcome these handicaps, communicate with the world, and spread her lectures promoting optimism. An inspiring read for everyone... *Biographies/Inspirational Pages 84*

Sara Crewe by **Frances Burnett** ISBN: *1-59462-360-0* **$9.45**
In the first place, Miss Minchin lived in London. Her home was a large, dull, tall one, in a large, dull square, where all the houses were alike, and all the sparrows were alike, and where all the door-knockers made the same heavy sound... *Childrens Classic Pages 88*

The Autobiography of Benjamin Franklin by **Benjamin Franklin** ISBN: *1-59462-135-7* **$24.95**
The Autobiography of Benjamin Franklin has probably been more extensively read than any other American historical work, and no other book of its kind has had such ups and downs of fortune. Franklin lived for many years in England, where he was agent... *Biographies/History Pages 332*

Name	
Email	
Telephone	
Address	
City, State ZIP	

☐ Credit Card   ☐ Check / Money Order

Credit Card Number	
Expiration Date	
Signature	

Please Mail to: Book Jungle
PO Box 2226
Champaign, IL 61825
or Fax to: 630-214-0564

ORDERING INFORMATION
web: *www.bookjungle.com*
email: *sales@bookjungle.com*
fax: *630-214-0564*
mail: *Book Jungle PO Box 2226 Champaign, IL 61825*
or PayPal *to sales@bookjungle.com*

Please contact us for bulk discounts

DIRECT-ORDER TERMS

20% Discount if You Order Two or More Books
Free Domestic Shipping!
Accepted: Master Card, Visa, Discover, American Express

www.ingramcontent.com/pod-product-compliance
Lightning Source LLC
Chambersburg PA
CBHW080542170426
43195CB00016B/2644